A gift of love and loyalty

Books by Lois Wyse

Nonfiction
Company Manners
The Six-Figure Woman
Lovetalk
Mrs. Success
"Funny, You Don't Look Like a Grandmother"
Kid, You Sing My Songs
Grandchildren Are So Much Fun
I Should Have Had Them First
Grandmother's Treasures
You Wouldn't Believe What My Grandchild Did
Women Make the Best Friends
Friend to Friend

Fiction
The Rosemary Touch
Far from Innocence
Kiss, Inc.
The Granddaughter
Seconds

Poetry
Love Poems for the Very Married
Are You Sure You Love Me?
A Weeping Eye Can Never See
Love Poems for a Rainy Day

Friend to Friend

Letters Only a Woman Could Write

A celebration of loyalty and love

LOIS WYSE

simon & schuster

Simon & Schuster
Rockefeller Center
1230 Avenue of the Americas
New York, NY 10020

SIMON & SCHUSTER and colophon are registered trademarks
of Simon & Schuster Inc.

Designed by BONNI LEON-BERMAN

Manufactured in the United States of America
1   3   5   7   9   10   8   6   4   2

Library of Congress Cataloging-in-Publication Data
Friend to friend : letters only a woman could write : a celebration of
loyalty and love / [compiled and edited by] Lois Wyse.
p.   cm.
Includes bibliographical references.
1. Women—Literary collections.   2. Women—Correspondence.
I. Wyse, Lois.
PN6071.W7F75   1997
808.86'082—dc21   97-672   CIP
ISBN 0-684-81168-5

The author gratefully acknowledges permission from the following
sources to reprint material in their control:
Elizabeth Barnett, literary executor to the estate of Edna St. Vincent Millay, for
lines from "Said the Little Lord Jesus to the Little Lord Buddha," copyright ©
1930 by Edna St. Vincent Millay. Excerpt from Letter No. 160 to Stephen Vincent
Benet and excerpt from Letter No. 159 to William Rose Benet from *Letters of Edna
St. Vincent Millay*, Harper & Row. Copyright © 1952, 1980 by Norma Millay Ellis.
All rights reserved. (continued on page 206)

For
The Wednesday Club
with love

C o n t e n t s

Introduction 15

I
C e l e b r a t i o n

"... your old friend ... will ... change to nobody knows who ..."
Harriet Beecher Stowe 25

"This letter seems to me very sentimental and I really mean it all. ..."
Anne Morrow Lindbergh 29

"I excessively hate to be forty ... I'm not ready yet."
Edith Wharton 33

"Dearest friend, To think that you are now a two months' wife,
& that I have never written ..."
Florence Nightingale 36

"What fun for all your friends, myself among them! ..."
Edna St. Vincent Millay 40

"Anyway, dear Hannah, I love him, more than before."
Mary McCarthy 44

"Now I have read the letter that only you could have written ..."
Rachel Carson 48

II
Appreciation

"I don't know what to write to you, so I shall tell you a story . . ."
Beatrix Potter   55

"Lord! how I liked you! how I rejoiced in your existence!"
Virginia Woolf   59

"I can thank you . . . for all the good there is in me . . ."
Louisa May Alcott   61

"Frankie, guess who came while you were away on vacation?
SAM PEPYS. Please thank whoever mailed him for me . . ."
Helene Hanff   64

"Gee we had a lovely time. Gosh we certainly do love you —"
Katy Dos Passos   68

"The physical distance between us now is longer
but not the basis of mental communion."
Mary Ritter Beard   73

"So thee sees that our Friends are thinking of us.
I was amazed at their generosity . . ."
Carol Zens Kellam   78

"Bless you for being so thoughtful and generous."
Joan Crawford   82

"Thank God for the money that you continue to send me . . ."
Jane Bowles   85

III
Consolation

"People always torture themselves in this way; I could do it, too, remembering that I hurt her, but instead I remember the happy times."
Edna St. Vincent Millay   93

"Your letter was a great comfort to me. I was kind of low. . . ."
Gertrude Stein   97

". . . it takes at least 10 years to realize the death of a parent . . ."
H.D.   101

". . . We are all so close together, Mother, and always will be —
life or death."
Anne Morrow Lindbergh   104

". . . no moment must be lost when a heart is breaking . . ."
Emily Dickinson   108

". . . to a friend that I am afraid of writing spontaneously."
Ayn Rand   112

"If one could only rid one's mind, completely of *words*
during the night, one would be better."
Dame Edith Sitwell   118

". . . we must go now, I to die, you to live."
Hannah Arendt   122

"You may say I long for death . . . but I long even more
to be cured."
Nancy Mitford   126

IV
The Ties that Bind

"... I received a Letter from my Friend ... it was a cordial
to my Heart."
Abigail Adams 133

"I just wanted you to know I am thinking of you and wish
I lived nearer."
Elizabeth Bishop 137

"To make a house is nothing. What is awful is to remake a house
after a crew of workmen have unmade it. ..."
Colette 141

"... you and my own sister are the three women who are tied to
my heart by a cord which can never be broken ..."
George Eliot 145

"Much love to David & a world of love to you Maude dear."
Eleanor Roosevelt 150

"... You ask if I really thought I could live in the house with two
men who were in love with me. ..."
M. F. K. Fisher 154

"... Now I'll tell you what to do ..."
Peg Bracken 158

"I wish I was this letter, so I could go in a plane
and be with you *quick*."
Dorothy Parker 163

". . . naturally she can't turn up back at work plus a baby . . ."
Dorothy Sayers 167

". . . I . . . long to lay my weary head somewhere and nestle my
full soul close to that of another in full sympathy—"
Susan B. Anthony 174

". . . I kept thinking of Iowa—of the cornhusking, the snow,
the sleighrides, the coasting, skating, the evenings with
stories and popcorn and nuts and apples . . ."
Elizabeth (Bess) Corey 177

". . . it would be impossible for me not to want you as a friend."
Flannery O'Connor 181

". . . never, never did I love you better, all my
beloved ones, than when I left you—"
Elizabeth Barrett Browning 184

"When [women] fail, then failure must be
but a challenge to others."
Amelia Earhart 190

"How you men wriggle and twist, and turn your backs
on all logic, before you will recognise the truth."
Clara Schumann 193

Postscript 197

Bibliography 203

13

we speak
but who remembers?

And so we write
To give memory to those thoughts
We want as legacy,
Those dreams we won't surrender,
And as we do
We retie the bonds that hold us
—And free us.

Introduction

*T*ucked away somewhere—perhaps in the drawer of a desk or tied with ribbon and secreted under hankies and sachets—are the letters of our lives.

These letters are our mileposts, our record of friendships and special times that burn bright in memory, tangible proof of lives that touched ours in ways so profound that someone cared enough to put feelings into written words.

We know and appreciate the thought and care that goes into letter writing. Haven't we all sat at one time or another, with blank stationery and frozen pen, struggling to find the right words to express feelings that must be shared, savored, preserved, and passed along to a friend?

In the course of our busy days there seems to be an ever-constant stream of phone calls, e-mail, and faxes to flood our lives with the often welcome—and sometimes rude—reminders of the good and the bad that awaits us beyond our four walls.

But a letter is a thing apart.

A letter is never ill-timed; it never interrupts. Instead it waits for us to find the opportune minute, the quiet moment to savor the message. There is an element of timelessness about letter writing; we are reminded of Jane Austen's novels and a more gracious way of life. Letter writing is that sweet surrender of time and place that allows us to recapture the essence of a particular closeness, when we recount those shared memories of special times and special people who have so enriched our lives.

There are as many reasons to send letters as there are excuses to put off writing them. We let life interrupt although we want to send a letter of congratulations or a follow-up note to someone we just met, a letter of sympathy, or even what a friend of mine calls "an act of presence"—those warming words sent when we want someone to know our thoughts are there, when we are aware that a friend needs a little bor-rowed courage.

Collected in this book are some of those written acts of presence, letters that are tangible proof of the best that friendship offers: solace, support, reasons to rejoice. And, as life would have it, there are also letters of grief, regret—even anger. Because they are all part of the chain of friendship, each is a link that bonds friend to friend. So even though each writer's life may vary from our own, these letters strike a res-onant chord because we share a timeless truth with these women. We know that we are all bound by the life stories we divulge to our friends, whether they be about the highs, the lows, or even the in-betweens of life.

We nod with sympathetic murmurs and accept the truth because we truly love each other, we women do.

We nurture each other through the seasons of growing up and growing old. In the beginning we send little notes in childish scrawl: "be my friend," "can you play after school?"

Later we graduate to the incessant telephoning of teen years, and we begin to let our friends in on the details of our lives. With those shared secrets we continually create and re-new the ties that bind friend to friend for life.

As we grow up and away, we stay in touch with old friends and collect new ones who reflect our changing lives and help define and mark the milestones in a woman's journey.

Still, despite the challenge and charm of new friends, we look back, sometimes wishing we could go back, sometimes relieved that certain parts of life will not be relived.

Sometimes our looking back is most poignant when we read our saved letters, even those sent long ago; frequently their message and sentiment remain as strong and vital today as when first we read them. And that is really what makes letters unique in the art of friendship; letters freeze time for us, eternalizing shared experiences so we can go back and draw strength from them. Letters are like deposits in a secret bank that can be withdrawn when they are needed. And as we look back in love, we appreciate anew the thought and time that was taken to express those feelings. The wellsprings of each woman's friendships run deep, and we plumb them with the reading of our letters. We are suffused with tender feelings and gratitude for those who paused long enough to write. In today's frenzied world we all know that it's possible to call a friend while doing three other things, but who ever wrote a letter while loading the dishwasher, programming the computer, or driving to the orthodontist?

Yet who ever regretted the time spent to reaffirm friendship?

Letters remind us that when we write we can bring back the best of times, even make time stand still, if only for a few minutes.

While many letters in this book were written years ago, some in other centuries, they remind us that even though the dates are old, the emotions expressed are fresh because they are repeated in successive generations.

The themes and sentiments are still as immediate for us today as when they were written, and so we are touched by long-ago letters that fairly dance off the page with joy, letters that detail a woman's travails, letters that track the deep commitment of true friendship and the distress when the relationship derails. And our hearts recognize a letter like that of Anne Morrow Lindbergh to her mother following the kidnapping and killing of Anne's son. Does that act of terrorism and the subsequent mourning not resonate in today's world of senseless, random death?

Most of the letters collected here were written by twentieth-century women because earlier there were few women's letters to save; frequently families did not bother to educate female children. Boys received schooling, and girls were given training in the domestic arts. Many letters before the twentieth century were written by daughters of the clergy. Girls raised in the parsonage often learned to read and write because scholarly debate and letter writing were part of family life; sometimes daughters learned by osmosis, but more often they were literate because their clerical fathers did not differentiate between the educational needs of boys and girls. Many of these educated girls grew up to be the chroniclers of family life, their letters forging the connections that touched the hearts and united disparate kin. Still others such as Harriet Beecher Stowe, the Brontës, and Louisa Mae Alcott sent their words far beyond their own families.

While a book cannot make a friendship, I hope that this one will strike a chord that reminds us to acknowledge our friends and the place they hold in our thoughts.

I hope readers will take these letters into their hearts so that the phrases and sentiments can be echoed in their lives.

With our letters and written words we tighten our circle, strengthen the links, one friend at a time, one link at a time.

Yet few of us find it easy to unfreeze the pen and fill the page. Elizabeth Bishop, long considered one of the major poets of the twentieth century, wrote to her friend Marianne Moore that there were "lots of things I'd like to say myself, and I'm trying to right now. I'll send you the results when I have done but I'm afraid they will strike you as pretty simpleminded. Well, they are sincere too—that's about all I can say for them."

And with a poet's true wisdom, Elizabeth Bishop succinctly gave the key to all our words and feelings of friendship: they are sincere.

I

Celebration

this old barn

Like the rafters of an old barn,
The roofbeams of friendship
Stay in place,
Held high and safe
By letters,
Our letters,
That protect us from the weathered world
Of time and space.

"...your old friend...
will...change to nobody
knows who..."

$\mathcal{B}$RIDES SELDOM FIND the velocity of words to keep pace with their feelings. Fears and fantasies commingle at a dizzying rate. Besides, who will listen?

Always a best friend.

Obviously Harriet Beecher knew that. And so, less than an hour before she was to be married, Harriet sat down and wrote a letter to one of her best friends.

That friend was Georgiana May (Harriet later named a daughter for her); the two girls formed their lifelong bond at the first women's school in the United States, Connecticut's

Litchfield Female Academy. Georgiana was described as "genius" with "the discretion, piety, energy, and steadiness that are seldom combined with genius."

History has proven the genius of Harriet Beecher Stowe, so it is small wonder that the strong-minded Harriet was attracted to Georgiana.

But the girls were separated—and one can imagine the sadness each felt—when Harriet and her siblings followed her father Lyman Beecher, a Congregational minister, from Hartford to Cincinnati, Ohio.

One of Harriet's first activities in Cincinnati was the formation of the Semi-Colon Club, a literary group that met in members' parlors and read one another the stories that they wrote. One of the Semi-Colon members was the widower Calvin Stowe, a well-educated man whose only personal property was a library of a thousand volumes. Despite his lack of worldly goods and only months after the death of his wife, Calvin Stowe found himself attached to Miss Beecher and proposed marriage.

Harriet, the competent young woman, suddenly found herself the flustered bride.

How Harriet must have longed to talk with Georgiana. The days before the wedding she was teary-eyed, sleepless, anxious.

And less than an hour before the wedding, now more composed than she had been for days, Harriet took pen in hand. . . .

January 6, 1836

Well, my dear G., about half an hour more and your old friend, companion, schoolmate, sister, etc., will cease to be Hatty Beecher and change to nobody knows who. My dear, you are engaged and pledged in a year or two to encounter a similar fate, and do you wish to know how you shall feel? Well, my dear, I have been dreading and dreading the time, lying awake all last week wondering how I should live through this overwhelming crisis, and lo! it has come and I feel *nothing at all.*

The wedding is to be altogether domestic; nobody present but my own brothers and sisters, and my old colleague, Mary Dutton; and as there is a sufficiency of the ministry in our family we have not even to call in the foreign aid of a minister. Sister Katy is not here, so she will not witness my departure from her care and guidance to that of another. None of my numerous friends and acquaintances who have taken such a deep interest in making the connection for me even know the day, and it will be all done and over before they know anything about it.

Well, it is really a mercy to have this entire stupidity come over one at such a time. I should be crazy to feel as I did yesterday, or indeed to feel anything at all. But I inwardly vowed that my last feelings and reflections on this subject should be yours, and as I have not got any, it is just as well to tell you that. Well, here comes Mr. S., so farewell, and for the last time I subscribe

Your own
H. E. B.

*"This letter seems to me
very sentimental and I really
mean it all...."*

*W*HEN SHE FELL in love, Anne Morrow knew she would be liberated from her conventional upbringing within a close family circle. But liberation came with an unexpected imprisonment of its own because marriage to a celebrity—and in his day, there was no celebrity to compare with the dashing prince of the air, Charles Lindbergh—meant the end to privacy.

Despite the hordes of photographers who followed their every move, the young Lindberghs managed to forge a deep bond of friendship. In addition, the new Mrs. Lindbergh maintained her own close friendships, particularly those with her family and early friends, friendships she reaffirmed regularly with long, reassuring letters. One of those early friends was Susanna Beck who, soon after Anne and Charles were married, wrote to tell Anne that she was now engaged to the archaeologist George C. Vaillant. The news so delighted Anne Morrow Lindbergh that she wrote this tender letter, a letter that only a loving wife could send to a cherished friend.

En route from Panama to Managua, October 5, 1929

Dear Sue,

I have completely given up hope of ever again sitting quietly at a desk and writing you the long pen-and-ink letter I have had in my mind for so long. I have been traveling literally ever since we were married and it is impossible to write in an open plane. Though strangely enough I have often felt in an open plane not as though I were writing a letter, but as though I were actually spending an afternoon with someone — one is so completely alone and apart and secure from interruptions. And I have told you exactly what I feel about your news. I hope it clicked in successful mutual telepathy!

Your letter reached me on one of the "off-again–on-again" stops in New York. It made me very very happy—first that you had told me about it, second because I think it perfect and inevitable and *right*. Sue, I just *glowed* for a whole week afterward with that news.

You said I would be shocked. I was surprised but with a surprise of recognition, if you see what I mean. You see, when we rode together you talked so much more of George than of anyone else, I remember thinking once or twice, "If I didn't know better I'd think she was in love with that man—that's the way I talk and think of C[harles]." Perhaps you don't realize how often you quoted George, or brought him into the conversation. And I loved it because I had met him and thought him one of the biggest, most vital and interesting men I had ever met. Naturally, he seemed a realer person than that rather dreamy, charming, introspective figure I had never met [a former attachment]. But I didn't say anything—I didn't want to stir up any indecision in your mind.

I hope you have that marvelous "swept out to sea" feeling that has complete faith and security underneath, because it does seem so right and wonderful to me. And believable. The people I care most about and think are "rare" *never* seem to marry other "rare" people. But you two are matched in "rareness" and "keenness" and "aliveness." (Do I sound like a maiden aunt congratulating you?)

Perhaps I know a little that conflict between the person who means sweetness and dearness and old association bound up with charm of place and time—a world very dear and lovely and . . . *safer*. And then the other: tremendous, overwhelming, and inevitable. But I am sure, sure, *sure* that the second is the soundest . . .

(This letter seems to me very sentimental and I really mean it all. Isn't it awful when your feelings, frozen into words, turn out to be sugar roses!)

"I excessively hate to be forty....
I'm not ready yet."

ALTHOUGH SHE DESCRIBED herself as "a self-made man," perhaps in defiance to critics who found her stories peculiarly unsentimental for a woman writer, Edith Wharton's life was marked by devoted friendships with women.

Among her first and dearest friends was Sara Norton. Such a logical friendship it was: Sara's father was the distinguished scholar Charles Eliot Norton and so he became Edith's literary father while Sara, his scholarly daughter, became her literary sister.

Throughout the more than twenty years of their correspondence, which ended only with Sara's death, the two women shared the news of their families and information about the books and authors who filled their lives. Because she trusted her friend's loyalty and judgment, Edith sought Sara's opinions about her writing. Sara, in turn, submitted her poetry to Edith as a fellow professional.

The friendship may well have informed some of the relationships between women that appeared in Edith Wharton's fiction. This letter was sent to Sara Norton by Edith Wharton as a response to Sara's having remembered one of those days of dread for many women: the fortieth birthday.

884 Park Avenue
January 24, 1902

Dear Sally,

How did you know anything about the "old-established" anniversary I am celebrating today? At any rate, your knowing, & your taking the trouble to send me that note, have given me more pleasure than anything else the day is likely to bring—I excessively hate to be forty. Not that I think it a bad thing to be—only I'm not ready yet!

Don't I know that feeling you describe, when one longs to go to a hospital and *have something cut out*, & come out minus an organ, but alive & active & like other people, instead of dragging on with this bloodless existence!! Only I fear you & I will never find a surgeon who will do us that service.

On Wednesday, at Mrs. Pat Campbell's play, I saw Mrs. Whitridge, who said she expected Miss Ward the next day. I hope I may see her, but I think it doubtful, as I go about so little.

Mrs. Campbell struck me the other night as a great ranting gawk. How I hate English & American acting. It's like an elephant walking on the keyboard of a piano.

While I had the "floo" I read Schopenhauer, not "en bloc," but the chapter on the ascetic life, which Mrs. Winty Chanler had spoken of as a marvellous analysis of the *état d'ame* of the saint. How strange it is rummaging in all that metaphysical lumber! —As for the sainthood, I prefer it as I find it in Pascal & St Francois de Sales —

I wish you were here & we could have a nice long talk.

Yr. devoted
E. W.

"Dearest friend,
To think that you are now
a two months' wife, & that
I have never written..."

$\mathcal{A}$LTHOUGH SHE WAS BORN into a life of privilege, she was also born into a family with liberal and humanitarian outlooks, so it is indeed fitting that her very name *Florence Nightingale* still stands for duty and sacrifice.

Florence, in her personal notes, just before her seventeenth birthday in 1837 reported that she had had a mystical experience and had been called by God to His service. Shortly thereafter she and her family left for a six-month tour of Europe. During that time she met Mary Clarke; "Clarkey" was brilliant, charming, and conducted one of the great salons of Paris. Even though she was twenty-seven years older than Florence the two became great friends and wrote often.

To Clarkey, Florence bared her deepest thoughts about love, marriage, and friendship (she thought too much energy went into all of them) and so interfered with the real goals of life.

In 1847 Florence wrote to Clarkey telling her she had seen a friend of hers, M. Mohl, in both London and Oxford. Florence said of the man ". . . . my opinion of him is, that he is thorough *Weltmensch*, who is labouring under a delusion (you know, they say we have all of us one mental delusion, some two—one monomania, which makes us think ourselves other than we are—in some it takes the form of conducting themselves as tea-pots, in others as Napoleons—one thinks himself a jug—another Jesus Christ) now my opinion of your friend is, that he thinks himself very much interested in the Civil Policy of England—whereas he is a thorough man of the world, who is very much bored by every thing but the things of Society."

To Florence, who had rejected Society by that time, having spurned suitors and decided that her call was to nursing, that was indeed a nineteenth century putdown.

So one can imagine that it was with mixed feelings of embarrassment and joy that she wrote only weeks later when her dear friend Clarkey married Julius Mohl, a brother of the disdained M. Mohl.

Dearest friend, To think that you are now a two months' wife, & that I have never written to tell you that your piece of news gave me more joy than I ever felt in all my life, except once, no, not even excepting that once, because *that* was a game of Blind-Man's-Buff, in *your* case you knew even as you were known. I had the news on a Sunday from dear Ju & and it was indeed a Sunday joy & I kept it holy. . . .

And now for my confessions. I utterly abjure, I entirely renounce & abhor, all that I may have said about M. Robert Mohl, not because he is now your brother-in-law, but because I was so moved & touched by the letters which he wrote after your marriage to Mama; so anxious they were to know more about you, so absorbed in the subject, so eager to prove to us that his brother was *such* a man, he was quite sure to make you happy.

And I have not said half enough either upon that score, not any thing that I feel; how 'to marry' is no impersonal verb, upon which I am to congratulate you, but depends entirely upon the accusative Case which it governs, upon which I do wish you heartfelt & trusting joy. In single life the stage of the Present & the Outward World is so filled with phantoms, the phantoms, not unreal tho' intangible, of Vague Remorse, Fears, dwelling on the threshold of every thing we undertake alone. . . . Yet . . . love still precedes joy . . .

But how impertinently I ramble on "You see a penitent before you," don't say, "I see an impudent scoundrel before me."; But when thou seest, & what more, when thou readest, forgive.

. . . And now, dearest friend, with *all* our *best* loves & congratulations to you & your Accusative or Nominative Case, believe me yours overflowingly, ever

yours,
Florence
Nightingale

*"What fun for all
your friends, myself
among them!..."*

ℰDNA ST. VINCENT MILLAY had talent, humor, and a flair for friendship. Her poetry touches the heart with its simple truths, and her humor is often discovered almost as a reader's surprise between the lines or in the off-beat endings to her bittersweet poems.

Her playful tone was evident in a Christmas card sent to friends in 1930:

> Said the little Lord Jesus to the little Lord Buddha,
> "The world is getting ruder and ruder."

Said the little Lord Buddha to the little Lord Jesus,
"They're only doing it to tease us."

In her everyday world Edna St. Vincent Millay did not tease. She set high standards for herself and her friends; and fellow writers often sought her opinions. She had no fear of telling a contemporary—with gentleness and supreme sensitivity—the reason she didn't like something. She once wrote to Edmund Wilson, whom she addressed as "Bunny," about a poem he sent her and said, "don't use the word—if it is a word—'gals.' Not even although it makes a fine Janus-faced rhyme for 'slag.' Don't do it. 'Slag' is a fine word. 'Gals' is cheap, common and indecent. Don't use it; don't for God's sake, use it, in a poem that has so much elegance."

Her critical judgment was used not only to find the lumps in literary puddings; she genuinely rejoiced when she thought that a writer and friend succeeded in creating a work of art. Steven Vincent Benét was a dear friend, and Millay's generosity as both a friend and a writer is apparent in this letter written to him on the publication of *John Brown's Body,* a major literary work that won a Pulitzer Prize.

Steepletop, Austerlitz, NY
Feb. 6, 1929

Dear Steve,

Can you forgive a non-union poet, who for weary months has been working twenty-two hours a day on her own stuff, for not writing to thank you for *John Brown's Body*, and to congratulate you upon a splendid piece of work? It made me so proud of you, Steve. And I don't know when I have been so happy about anything as I have been about the success of this book of yours—I mean its success from every point of view, not just that it's so darned good, but that so many people think so, and are buying it. What fun for you and Rosemary! What fun for all your friends, myself among them! And what fun for me to write to the Guggenheims as I had occasion to do the other day in answer to a letter such as they once wrote me regarding you: And what did I tell you once about Steve Benét—and wasn't I right?

Dear Children: I have just-reread the above, and I see that it sounds rather as if I were proud of myself, than proud of you. It sounds as if it were written with the thumbs in the weskit-armholes. And although you know that it wasn't written like that—since who could type with any fluency and his thumbs in his armholes?—still I feel that I must hasten to tell you that this is not the case. I haven't seen you for a long time.

I wonder if you remember me clearly enough to be sure how happy I am for you.

. . . I suppose you are hard at work on another big book now, Steve. I wonder what it is going to be. Whatever it is, I know it is something I shall love to read. I thought some of the lyrics in *John Brown's Body* were among your loveliest. I adored the one about the Hilders, and the one that says: Now listen to me, you Tennessee corn.

Good luck to you, and happiness, and all the things you want. And my love to you both.

Jerry*

*Edna St. Vincent Millay sometimes used different names in signing her letters, depending on the circumstances.

"Anyway, dear Hannah,
I love him, more than before."

WHO KNOWS WHEN or how her love will be found?

For some it comes walking through the garden gate. Others bump into it on the subway, and in this case she simply looked up over a teacup in a small café and was smitten.

How was Mary McCarthy, thrice-married and on a holiday tour of Prague and Vienna with her third husband and son by her second marriage, to know that the longest love of her life would begin December 29, 1959, when her party was met in Warsaw by James Raymond West, the Public Affairs Officer at the U.S. Embassy?

Two weeks later, West told McCarthy he wanted to

marry her. There were, of course, a few problems—she already had a husband, and he had not only a wife but three children.

By April, McCarthy had returned to the United States, told her husband she was going back to Europe—and to West. Then, as women the world over do when they're early in love, Mary McCarthy reached out to talk things over with a best friend.

That friend, with whom she had a remarkable twenty-five-year correspondence, was Hannah Arendt, the philosopher who had fled Nazi Germany, and whose penetrating intelligence matched Mary McCarthy's. Through their letters the women shared the good, the bad, and the imponderable.

And yes, Mary McCarthy and James West did marry; the marriage lasted twenty-eight years—until her death in 1989.

Hotel d'Inghilterra
Via Bocca di Leone 14
Roma
April 20, 1960

Dearest Hannah:
Here is the "Arrived safe" letter—a little late because I didn't get back from Vienna till last night. . . .

I want to tell you this much about Jim. It was a somber time (ours) in part, or chequered like the Vienna weather. He has been through a sort of hell in Warsaw (which he hadn't told me) with that woman (his wife) and the sight of the children. . . . Coming home at night for their bedtime, then going back to the Embassy to work till midnight or one, working in the same way weekends and having a sandwich and whiskey and soda or a coffee for dinner, so as not be at home with her. Or, when she was out, eating alone in the dining room. Sleeping on the divan. Because she will not have the furniture moved around, so that the little girl could sleep in her room and he in the little girl's; it would cause talk among the Embassy servants, she says. In the mornings, he and the children tiptoe around in the dark, so as not to disturb mamma, who is sleeping. . . . When he got to Vienna, he suddenly discovered he was totally exhausted by this daily torture—all nerves; the second morning he abruptly wept for a minute or two. This doesn't mean a lessening of love; on the contrary, a hardening of determination. What he has been doing, in Warsaw, is confront, very grimly, the price, and the price is the children, whom he loves. He insists on seeing this clearly, without softening it. ("You will have them for the summer anyway," or "Maybe we can take all three of them, in time, or one at least"; these assurances, from me, don't palliate anything for him.) On the other hand, he *will* not live with her; the damage to the children, some of it, has already been done or was done at their birth. "I keep reminding myself," he says, sadly laughing, "that *I* asked that girl to marry me." While we were in Vienna, we drew up a sort of settlement plan. . . .

Anyway, dear Hannah, I love him, more than before. He's the most wholly serious person I've ever known, anywhere; I don't mean lacking in gayety or human or wild high spirits. It is way beyond thinking about the pros and cons or having doubts; it's simply a fact. And I'm glad. . . .

Love and kisses
to you,
Mary

*"Now I have read
the letter that only you could
have written . . ."*

$\mathcal{A}$PPROPRIATELY THIS FRIENDSHIP began with a letter. When Dorothy Freeman, then fifty-five, learned that the best-selling author Rachel Carson, forty-six, was to become her neighbor at Southport Island, Maine, she wrote a welcoming note because Dorothy and her husband Stanley, longtime admirers of Rachel's work, had read her book aloud to one another.

Even though this friendship began with a love of the sea, it contracted—and grew—from the greatness of natural wonder to the immediacy of the daily lives of both women.

Dorothy and Rachel wrote frequently, for even though they saw little of one another, their dreams and hopes, as well as their concerns and despairs, were mirrored in their letters, letters that created the intimate atmosphere in which each found comfort; letters that had a profound effect on their relationship. Early in their correspondence Rachel wrote, ". . . the necessity of writing instead of speaking [may] have contributed to the depth of love and understanding that have developed."

Rachel's artistic life was often interrupted by considerations for those in her family she served as both breadwinner and caretaker. Dorothy had a husband, son, grandchildren, and household of her own to manage.

Still each managed to treat her letter-writing with a thoughtful love. Although Rachel used a typewriter for manuscripts, her letters to Dorothy were always written on carefully chosen, pretty notepaper in pale shades of blue, green, or cream. Dorothy, too, wrote her long letters by hand. Occasionally one or the other of the letter writers would include a flower from her garden in the missive.

As a tribute to their friendship, Rachel dedicated her book *The Edge of the Sea* to the Freemans. As a publication gift, Dorothy and Stanley gave Rachel a diamond pin in the shape of a seashell along with a letter of thanks.

In response, while en route to New York, Rachel wrote the following letter to Dorothy.

October 25, 1955

Now I have read the letter that only you could have written. I waited until we could be alone together on the train, and it has been sweet to have you traveling with me. I had wanted to write you a little message for tomorrow, also, to hand to you at the party tonight, and although writing on a speeding train is not what I would have chosen, I think I'm glad I have waited until I had read your precious note. . . . if one can assume anything so unthinkable as to suppose I did not know why I had dedicated the book to you . . . it is because there is no one else like you in my life — now or ever . . . The one thing I wish today above all else is that as the years pass we may never come to take for granted this beautiful sympathy and understanding that exist between us, but may always feel their shining wonder as we do today.

. . . I am glad [this dedication] makes you happy . . . But for me, too, there is deep happiness that I have been given friends so dear and precious to me that I could feel as I do about the dedication — so completely satisfied with its rightness . . .

Rachel

II

Appreciation

Duty has its own demands,
And we women
Who nurse the needs
Of those we love
Do what we must
And often trust
That somewhere someone
Smiles in silent satisfaction.

Yet when the silence is broken
By a written word that shows
That someone knows,
We willingly pour cups of joy
In thanks for thanks.

"I don't know what
to write to you, so I shall
tell you a story . . ."

WHEN BEATRIX POTTER was seventeen, Annie Carter
came to live with the Potter family as both Beatrix's companion and teacher of German. Since Annie was Beatrix's senior
by only three years, the two young women found they had
much in common and formed a fast friendship. Even after
Annie married and left the Potters' employ, the two young
women stayed in close touch, and their unique and loving
friendship continued to flourish.

They conversed easily and often, and as their friendship
reached new levels of trust and understanding, Beatrix

came to care for Annie's children as fondly as she cared for Annie.

When Annie's four-year-old son Noel became ill, Beatrix wanted to reach out and help her friend. Although Beatrix had no children of her own to guide her in the ways of diverting a young boy, she drew on her own childhood memories and, out of friendship for Annie and her family, wrote this letter to Noel.

Undoubtedly it cheered him just as it has cheered generations of children ever since.

September 2, 1893

My dear Noel,

I don't know what to write to you, so I shall tell you a story about four little rabbits whose names were Flopsy, Mopsy, Cottontail and Peter.

They lived with their mother in a sand bank under the roof of a big fir tree.

"Now my dears," said old Mrs. Bunny, "you may go into the field on down the lane, but don't go into Mr. McGregor's garden."

Flopsy, Mopsy and Cottontail, who were good little rabbits, went down the lane to gather blackberries, but Peter, who was very naughty ran straight away to Mr. McGregor's garden and squeezed underneath the gate.

First he ate some lettuce and some broad beans, then some radishes, and then, feeling rather sick, he went to look for some parsley; but round the end of a cucumber frame, whom should he meet but Mr. McGregor!

Mr. McGregor was planting out young cabbages, but he jumped up and ran after Peter carrying a rake and calling out, "Stop, thief."

Peter was most dreadfully frightened and rushed all over the garden, for he had forgotten the way back to the gate. He lost one of his shoes among the cabbages and the other shoe among the potatoes. After losing them he ran on four legs and went faster, so that I think he would have got away altogether if he had not unfortunately run into a gooseberry net and got caught fast by the large buttons on his jacket. It was a blue jacket with brass buttons, quite new.

Mr. McGregor came up with a basket which he intended to pop on the top of Peter, but Peter wriggled out just in time, leaving his jacket behind, and this time he found the gate, slipped underneath and ran home safely.

Mr. McGregor hung up the little jacket and shoes for a scarecrow, to frighten the blackbirds.

Peter was ill during the evening, in consequence of overeating himself. His mother put him to bed and gave him a dose of camomile tea, but Flopsy, Mopsy and Cottontail had bread and milk and blackberries for supper.

I am coming back to London next Thursday, so I do hope I shall see you soon, and the new baby. I remain, dear Noel, yours affectionately

Beatrix Potter

*"Lord! how I liked you!
how I rejoiced
in your existence!"*

FROM THE MOMENT they met, Virginia Woolf knew it was going to be a friendship that mattered. But then she was a woman of passion, and her passions spilled over into her writing and through her life.

So when Virginia Woolf met Ethel Smith, a composer, Virginia's own sense of adventure and intuition prompted her to believe that Ethel would become one of the critical friends in her life. And the two women did become close friends.

After their first meeting, Virginia wrote a letter so full of life and love and joy that even rereading it generations later, one wishes the party and the friendship were still going on.

July 1930

I say Ethel—what a party! What a triumph! . . . I daresay it went on for hours after we left in the garden, under the roses. It was a superb affair, rolling and warbling from melody to melody like some divine quartet—no, octet. First the meeting; then the golf; then the returning; then the supper, and all interwoven with so many extraneous melodies, to me so fascinating; Lady Balfour, Mrs. Lyttleton and then the champagne and then—oh millions of other things which I noticed at the time, but had hardly leisure to taste . . . Lord! how I liked you! how I rejoiced in your existence! We are still talking it over, and saying, "Do you remember the other night at Ethel's"—or "Did you notice how . . ." and so on. By the way, Leonard was more overcome than I've known him by any party these ten years. . . .

"I can thank you . . .
for all the good there is in me . . ."

$\mathcal{S}$HE WAS A girl raised as few young nineteenth-century women were brought up. The daughter of the educator and philosopher Bronson Alcott, little Louisa met the best and brightest of her time in her own home. Ralph Waldo Emerson and Henry David Thoreau tutored her.

But, as everyone who ever read *Little Women* is aware, the life she lived with her family influenced her as much—or more—than her esteemed tutors.

Her mother was a best friend, and her sisters were best friends, too. Even as biographers detail the strong men who guided Louisa May Alcott, they often fail to mention the mother she loved so dearly and who was obviously the model for Mother March.

Louisa demonstrated her great love and appreciation for her mother when she gave her first publication, *Flower Fables*, as a Christmas present with the winsome suggestion that it was Louisa's first child and therefore her mother's grandchild.

But biographers have not written of the love and friendship between mother and daughter—and so it remains, like Louisa's new-found novels, to be discovered here in her letter of appreciation and devotion with her first published book.

20 Pinckney Street
Boston
December 24, 1854

Dear Mother,

Into your Christmas stocking I have put my "firstborn," knowing that you will accept it with all its faults (for grandmothers are always kind), and look upon it merely as an earnest of what I may yet do; for, with so much to cheer me on, I hope to pass in time from fairies and fables to men and realities.

Whatever beauty or poetry is to be found in my little book is owning to your interest and encouragement of all my efforts from the first to the last; and if ever I do anything to be proud of, my greatest happiness will be that I can thank you for that, as I may do for all the good there is in me, and I shall be content to write if it gives you pleasure.

Jo is fussing about;
My lamp is going out.

To dear mother, with many kind wishes for a happy New Year and merry Christmas.

> I am your ever
> loving daughter
> Louy

*"Frankie, guess who came
while you were away on vacation?
SAM PEPYS. Please thank
whoever mailed him for me..."*

EPISTOLARY FRIENDSHIPS ARE the unwitting victims of Marconi, Bell, and, most recently, Bill Gates. No longer do many of us regularly converse in print, revealing our secrets and dreams to our friends and sharing our visions of the future in letters that will be long treasured.

One of the truly great epistolary friendships was that between New York writer Helene Hanff and used-book dealer Frank Doel, in London. Their friendship was celebrated in a 1970 publication of their letters titled *84, Charing Cross Road*. It still charms readers of all ages. For many years I wrote a column for *Good Housekeeping* magazine and frequently listed some of my favorite books along with those chosen by my readers. Even twenty-five years after its original publication, readers listed Helene Hanff's as a favorite. Because of the book's popularity I went to visit Ms. Hanff one afternoon and found her to be as feisty and bright as one would expect from her letters.

The original correspondence with Mr. Doel, who was employed by Marks & Co. (sadly, it's no longer in business) began with a query from an avowed Anglophile, Miss Hanff, who responded to a store ad in *The Saturday Review of Literature*. Although Miss Hanff had never been to England, she kept up a steady correspondence with Mr. Doel and came to know his staff and family from 1949 to 1969 as their letters continued. It was not until the English publication of *84, Charing Cross Road* that Helene Hanff finally went to London. By then Frank Doel had died, so she never met the man who changed her life letter by letter. This letter is typical of the high-spirited, slightly irreverent missives she wrote. She was often playful in addressing the man she never met but came to know so well. Doel's letters were more reserved and respectful. But Helene Hanff wrote with cheerful abandon; their mutual love of literature freed her spirit and loosened her pen.

14 East 95th St.
New York City
September 18, 1952

Frankie, guess who came while you were away on vacation? SAM PEPYS! Please thank whoever mailed him for me, he came a week ago, stepped out of four pages of some tabloid, three honest navy-blue volumes of him; I read the tabloid over lunch and started Sam after dinner.

He says to tell you he's overJOYED to be here, he was previously owned by a slob who never even bothered to cut the pages. I'm wrecking them, it's the thinnest India paper I ever saw. We call it "onion skin" over here and it's a good name for it. But heavier paper would have taken up six or seven volumes so I'm grateful for the India. I only have three bookshelves and very few books left to throw out.

I houseclean my books every spring and throw out those I'm never going to read again like I throw out clothes I'm never going to wear again. It shocks everybody. My friends are peculiar about books. They read all the best sellers, they get through them as fast as possible. I think they skip a lot. And they NEVER read anything a second time so they don't remember a word of it a year later. But they are profoundly shocked to see me drop a book in the wastebasket or give it away. The way they look at it, you buy a book, you read it, you put it on the shelf, you never open it again for the rest of your life but YOU DON'T THROW IT OUT! NOT IF IT HAS A HARD COVER ON IT! Why not? I personally can't think of anything less sacrosanct than a bad book or even a mediocre book.

Trust you and Nora [his wife] had a fine holiday. Mine was spent in Central Park, I had a month's vacation from joey, my dear little dentist, he went on his honeymoon. i financed the honeymoon. Did I tell you he told me last spring I had to have all my teeth capped or all my teeth out? I decided to have them capped as I have got used to having teeth. But the cost is simply astronomical. So Elizabeth will have to ascend the throne without me, teeth are all I'm going to see crowned for the next couple of years.

i do NOT intend to stop buying books, however, you have to have SOMEthing. Will you see if you can find me Shaw's dramatic criticism please? and also his music criticism? I think there are several volumes, just send whatever you can find, now listen, Frankie, it's going to be a long cold winter and I baby-sit in the evenings AND I NEED READING MATTER, NOW DON'T START SITTING AROUND, GO FIND ME SOME BOOKS.

hh

"Gee we had a lovely time. Gosh we certainly do love you —"

THANK-YOU LETTERS often sound like exercises in etiquette, but in the hands of a gifted writer, a thank-you note can sound like a good short story. Although John Dos Passos, not Katy, was the more well-known writer in the family, it was Katy who wrote chatty, bright, and loving letters to friends. Most notable among the friends were Sara and Gerald Murphy, whose friendships formed and informed much of the writing of many important American authors in the 1930s and 1940s. Sara Murphy was described as a woman comfortable with herself, both loving and generous as a friend. The men and women of their generation cared deeply for Gerald but loved Sara unconditionally.

In describing the comfort level with Sara, John Dos Passos said that with Sara "you never lack the right cushion in your chair." Her ability to offer cheer and coziness to the people she knew made friends of them all, but when she truly cared for them, they became her friends for life. She once said to Ernest Hemingway, "You don't *really* think I am snooty do you? Please don't. It isn't snooty to choose. Choice, and one's affections, are about all there are. And I am rather savage, like you about first—best everything: best painting, best music, best friends. I'd rather spend a few hours a year with the friends I love than hundreds with indifferents."

So it is not surprising that her literate, amusing, interesting, first-rate friends managed to thank her with words she would have thought "first."

Provincetown, 15 January 1938

Dearest Mrs. Puss,

Oh Mrs. Puss your hooked rugs are down on our floor and we are walking on them proud as princes on plush. They look wonderful and feel as fine underfoot—have a cosey warm look too, very grateful in this weather. There's a deep

snow and the sea is a clear black with little crisps of ice at the edges. I wish you were here. We are crazy to know how you liked the tropical isle (Jamaica?). Your cards sounded as if you did like it. Did you notice the Indian cattle—of course you did, and I'm sure that Mr. Puss saw more than anyone ever did—he always does. I often wish Mr. Puss were President. "Mr. Puss for President!" Make a fine election slogan, wouldn't it? He could go right in and straighten out the State Department. I am sure they are in a terrible way with their files. Darling we miss you both, and Miss Puss too—hope to see you about the middle of next week—We're coming down for a protracted stay of two or three weeks—Have to hole up at the Lafayette, as Dos is working like a mule train—But we can come in every day and nag you.

I hate to leave—it's been so lovely here—we take great walks on the sunny hills every day—it's been like Spring till this snow—Then we come in for a drink at five o'clock—and there are the hooked rugs, simply glowing on the floor—Mrs. Puss-cat dear, thank you so much. I don't think I managed to tell you how we enjoyed the little Arabian nights house in East Hampton—My, that's a lovely house—Gee we had a lovely time. Gosh we certainly do love you—

We have Charley Kaeselau's little boy staying here. He's just out of the hospital—an operation on his leg, and is still in a plaster cast. An attractive clever child, but very spoiled and bad—He has two favorite replies—One is No. The other is I hope you choke. I have broken him of the last retort which was really rather trying. But what do you do when you tell a child to do something and he looks at you darkly and says No. He kicks when he's put to bed. What do you do then?

Have you heard from Pauline [Hemingway]? I suppose Ernest is in Spain now, with the big Teruel fight going on. It's a sensational victory—the greatest of the whole war, and must mean that Franco is badly crippled, as now he can't push his offensive except under terrific difficulties.

. . . We had two great Xmas parties, much larger than we intended. We gave two, so we would not have too many people at a time, but all the people we didn't invite came anyway, both times, so nothing was gained by it. Dos made his old father's rum punch the first time but that turned out to be a mistake, as it went to people's heads, so we made egg-nog the second time, but that was a mistake too as they just got into the cellar and drank straight whiskey. They had the oddest reasons for asking for the whiskey. One boy said he had appendicitis — Another said he couldn't touch egg-nog because of his diabetes, another claimed he was allergic to cream and eggs . . .

. . . Dos and I don't know where we are going. Maybe to Texas. But first to New York where we'll see you and that's the best of the New Year to date.

1938 Love,
Katy

"The physical distance between us now is longer but not the basis of mental communion."

$\mathcal{M}$ARY RITTER BEARD was the less well-known member in her lifelong professional and personal collaboration with Charles A. Beard. Famed as historians, both husband and wife worked to include women in the telling of history or, as Mary Beard preferred to say, the history of civilization.

In her view the whole social fabric was not woven without women's strands. She was not interested in sexual equality so long as it meant conforming to a male norm; instead she devoted her efforts to equal rights.

With her husband, Mary Beard wrote textbooks on

United States' history; yet despite her contributions to the partnership, she never sought the limelight for herself.

Because she and her husband spent so much of their life together, the Beards exchanged few letters. After her husband's death, however, Mary Beard wrote to her son: "As for my being free now, I have had as much freedom all along as I really cared for . . . I loved sitting at home with my darling every night and being at his side all the days . . . Outsiders . . . could not fully comprehend our mutual happiness in working, jabbering and getting such exercise as we took in our simple ways. THIS IS AN ABSOLUTE TRUTH."

The letter that follows was written to a woman who, like Mary Beard, had a husband more famous than she. The woman was Luella Gettys, and her husband was the political scientist V. O. Key. Mrs. Beard's willingness to move into the background so long as her husband had the floor is obvious in almost all her letters; indeed self-abnegation, next to scholarship, seems to be her outstanding characteristic.

For Mary Beard friendship began with shared commitment; if that did not exist at the start, nothing could exist later.

New Milford—Connecticut
April 25, 1941

Dear Luella Gettys:

You are a "prolific" writer and editor but that is not the whole story of your writing.

Thanks without stint—and not as a "stint"—for sending me your opuses, many-paged, and in pamphlet form. Your subjects are important. You write with scholarly care. If I had read my *Political Science Review* in the library at the Hopkins, I would have been familiar with your Canadian Federalism article before I left Baltimore, but we had not had our magazines forwarded during the winter and only now have we begun to catch up with this *Review*. Anyway I like Reprints and am so glad to have yours.

Having worked to get the legislation which provides more security for American women married to foreigners, your study of the large question of Naturalization means much to me as the larger if inclusive question.

You have the training and mind of a scholar. I am a blunderbuss by comparison. But I am daring to send you a copy of one of my blunderings through the maze of history searching for Woman. I have to be honest and mark the errata before you read it. They show me up horribly as a too-ready-to-print gal. But what I print has to be rushed along to get anything of my very own out between orgies of co-authorship with CAB. The orgies have a pleasure all their own and so do the separate thrusts at self-expression, though in the individual case I am more embarrassed by the weaknesses of the outcome.

Longmans, Green promised me that I could have a new edition of the book I am sending you, to appear late in 1941. I prepared the revision and, with their consent, ironed out all the signs of sex resentment which appear in the copy you are getting. I had changed the title to indicate that I was trying to review history and the new edition was announced in mid-autumn of last year as *Woman: Co-Maker of History.* But I had opened with a current story of women's helping to make war—today and through the yesterdays. That is not a marketable proposition at this hour of history and the publishers did not like the new opening. So the revision is in cold storage, as I am sure I told you. My main regret is that it had corrected all the errors which appear, marked, in the copy I am sending you. Anyway I have the right to get another publisher and, with longer time for improvement, the better book will be on the market some day.

The physical distance between us now is longer but not the basis of mental communion. I cannot say that I have attained the scholarship which would eliminate the mental distance but I can say that I appreciate exceeding care, caution, and that kind of reportage.

I think CAB will look less like an "asphalt flower" next week when he lectures again at the Hopkins. It will be better for him when he no longer has to climb all those stairs to his office, for when one is nearing the seventies the heart usually resists that particular kind of strain. Yet perhaps the heart follows the leadership of the mind (*pace* Christian Scientists) and forgets to palpitate itself when the mind decides that what it is attempting is supremely worth while. Best wishes to you and "V. O.". . .

"So thee sees that our Friends
are thinking of us.
I was amazed at their generosity . . ."

WAR, THE MEANS by which nations try to settle differences and cause the unsettling of families, was the glue that bound America in the 1940s.

World War II was probably the reason for more letter writing than any previous generation of Americans had experienced. Schoolchildren wrote to recent graduates; neighbors sent packages and letters; mothers and wives wrote daily; young girls wrote to soldiers they were parted from. Indeed, letter writing became the patriotic thing to do, the best way the home front could keep up the spirits of the boys at the war front.

And "the boys" were on everyone's minds. Were they safe? Were they alive? How were the Allies doing?

Only a small group of citizens did not march to the wartime drums. Of the 34 million men who registered for the draft, approximately 72,000 declared themselves conscientious objectors and asked for exemption from military service. Most requests were granted, and some COs did serve on battlefronts in noncombative service.

Six thousand persons, however, were not given conscientious objector status and were imprisoned. One of them was John Kellam, a city planner in Toledo, Ohio, who had married Carol Zens in the early 1940s after the two met at a Society of Friends meeting in Washington, D.C.

John had applied for CO status before joining the Society of Friends, whose tenets include pacifism. When he was called to service in 1944, he refused induction. On Christmas Eve he was arrested by the FBI; in January 1945, he was convicted, fined $1,000, and sentenced to five years in prison.

Carol was pregnant by then and went back to Washington, D.C., to live with her mother. This letter was sent to John by Carol during his imprisonment. After his release from the Lewisburg Federal Prison, John and Carol moved to Providence, Rhode Island, where he became a city planner.

But during troubled times, what can matter more than friendship shown to a family out of step and out of favor with society?

Washington, D.C., July 19, 1945

My Dearest:

... The Friends had a shower for me at the Meeting House, Sunday afternoon, July 8. I received many lovely gifts for the baby. . . . The Meeting House Friends are giving me a high chair and more than enough money for the doctor's bill and for two months' diaper-washing service. Allen said there was no collection taken—that people had been asking him if they couldn't help in some way, so he had just let them know about the shower. So thee sees that our Friends are thinking of us. I was amazed at their generosity toward us, and didn't know what to say, but I appreciate their thoughtfulness very, very much.

I had this letter from thy Mom, dated July 12: "Thank you, thank you, for relieving my mind about John. I knew that something was very wrong and I kept thinking that perhaps he was being a 'guinea pig' of some sort, and it was driving me crazy. Please don't encourage any more 'sacrifice,' will you? He has an immediate duty to you and me and to his child, which is more important than any so-called sacrificial expression of Spirit. I warned him about hunger strikes or other demonstrations of martyr complexes, before I left him. . . . I shall continue to pray that he be kept safe and well in body and mind and spirit . . ."

I didn't think it would do much harm to tell her of thy hunger strike after it was all over and thee was recovering so nicely. I didn't expect her to be so concerned, but I can understand why she should be. Does thee think thee can write to her and Alex?

All my love to
thee, darling,
Thy Cary.

"Bless you for being so thoughtful and generous."

$\mathcal{S}$HE WON AN Academy Award, more than a few men lost their hearts to her, and ultimately she became a successful businesswoman representing Pepsi-Cola (her last husband, the dynamic Alfred Steele, was the company president). But Joan Crawford is probably best remembered today as the cruel mother described in the devastating biography titled *Mommie Dearest*. To her friends, however, Joan Crawford was gentle and charming even as she played her life's role as The Ultimate Movie Star.

Peter Rogers, now well-known as a painter and photographer, became one of those friends when he induced Crawford to pose in a mink coat for the advertising series he produced titled "What Becomes a Legend Most." After that the two became good friends. "She was the ultimate movie star," Rogers recalls. "When she came to the door she might look like a simple hausfrau, but within minutes she would excuse herself and return in full makeup and wearing glamorous clothes. She was always gracious, always considerate and, surprisingly, always appreciative of any gift or note. I have a series of letters and cards from her, and each is almost old-fashioned in its propriety. Whenever I was her guest, I sent flowers, books or records, and she responded with notes that reflected the meticulous aspect of her personality: she always mentioned every flower in the arrangement or repeated the titles of the books and their authors or the recordings and the soloists, almost as if she wanted to be certain that I understood that in her thanks she took as much care as I did in the selection.

"Publicly her daughter chose to castigate her, but to so many of us who called her 'friend,' she was memorable for her kindness and sincerity."

This letter is from Mr. Rogers's collection.

March 27, 1971

Peter dear,

How very good of you to give me the book, *Women in Love,* by D. H. Lawrence, for my birthday. It is just what I wanted—and I am so happy to have it. It was so dear of you to remember that I wanted not only to see the picture but to read the book as well. Bless you for being so thoughtful and generous. You helped to make my birthday a very joyous one.

My love to you—and I'll be seeing you soon.

As ever,
Joan

"Thank God for the money that you continue to send me . . ."

WHEN SHE WAS young she corresponded with a swift pen and an irresistible charm.

There was a nervous energy to her friendships and to all her life actions. She seemed to live at top speed; perhaps she sensed early on that it was to be a short life.

Jane Bowles was far from a household name; her husband Paul was far better-known. Perhaps she, too, would have had more fame, but at the age of forty, Jane suffered a stroke and never truly regained her powers of speech and thought.

In good times (they once went to Cuba together on a holiday) and in bad times, Libby Holman remained a true friend to Jane. Libby, a popular singer in the 1930s and 1940s, gave her friend money when she needed it and lent support during those times when Jane was frightened and almost incoherent. Because they were rarely in the same place at the same time, the two friends wrote to one another frequently, reaffirming their love and, in Libby's case, offering continuing assistance which Jane deeply appreciated—and needed.

And because the friendship was so close, Jane was willing to admit her fears and despair to Libby.

Tangier, Morocco
May 10, 1966

Darling Libby,

My plans are at a virtual standstill. I don't know what to do. Martha [Princess Martha Ruspoli de Chambrun] who was, I thought, going to go over to America with me—and come back as well—is now putting off her trip untill the fall. She says she will deffinitely go back with me in the fall because she needs to in order to keep up her residence in the

U.S. . . . Libby, my spelling worries me so much that I am afraid to come home and see what is wrong with me that wasn't wrong with me before. Maybe some premature deterioration due to the original stroke. I don't know. I don't know what is physical any longer and what is mental. I hoped always that I would get better but it does not look that way (the spelling), does it? I am frightfully depressed and I don't know how I can start off alone . . . If there is anything wrong with me then I'm sure it's so bad that nothing will help it, and if there isn't then I suppose it must be some reaction to all these years of drugs. I hope so. My book, *Two Serious Ladies*, I made no money at all or to be exact about four hundred dollars since publication including the advance. It is at the same time considered To be a literary success in certain circles which I never get into since I am not there, I am here. I don't know if I ever sent you the book or whether or not we decided that it was useless because you had read it. Perhaps we decided that you should have a copy in order to lend it to friends. I don't know. My memory is so bad because of my stroke and the premature senility that resulted that I keep forgetting everything. At the same time if you saw me you would notice that I am still charming and seem very bright and even young. I am horribly worried about myself but on certain days I am less . . . Thank God for the money that you continue to send me . . . The money means a lot to me. If someday it doesn't I will let you know at once so that it can be free for someone else —

I have Paul available today to correct the spelling of this

letter and so I will wait until he gets down here. I have thought, as you know, about sending the letter without corrections but I think Paul would be horrified and ashamed for you to see so many mistakes, and you yourself could be depressed.

. . . I hope to God that you have written though I deserve not to hear for awhile . . .

Lee Gershwin was here and gave me a very modern tiny slip for skirts that are above the knees. Naturally I could not wear a skirt above the knee with my leg but I love the baby slip. My slips are more like slips for a concert pianist. I was upset about the Leary scandal which Paul heard about from Susan Sontag, whom you've surely met or at least heard of. Much love to the whole family and please write me.

Jane

III

Consolation

old words read like new

Today I needed you
And so I called.
    rrrrrrring—
    no answer

Rummaging in memory,
  I then recalled
  Your long-ago letter
  Written to address my doubts.
  Strange—but your old words
  Read like new
  —and once again you saved me.

> *"People always torture themselves in this way; I could do it, too, remembering that I hurt her, but instead I remember the happy times."*

IT ALL BEGAN when they were both afloat in New York in the twenties. It was a time for burning candles at both ends—and both Elinor and Edna, while pursuing their literary lives, managed to break more than a few hearts and to flout more than a few conventions.

Their friendship was a celebrated one because Greenwich Village in those days was a very small community, and the literati reigned. And what women were more well-known than Edna St. Vincent Millay and Elinor Wylie, the sonateers of bittersweet love?

When Elinor divorced Andrew Wylie, Edna was there

for her; and Edna lent her support when Elinor married Edna's good friend, the writer William Rose Benét. Even though Elinor was never one to be satisfied with what she had and looked always to what might have been, Edna remained true to her friend—and continued to listen.

Once, four years after her marriage to Benét, Elinor wrote to Wylie telling him ". . . I am going to admit to you that I wish with all my heart I had never left you . . ."

Edna knew this—and more. Still Edna and her husband, the Dutch-born businessman Eugen Boissevain, remained dear friends with the Benéts and during the five years of the Benét marriage, the four spent memorable times at Steepletop, the home Edna and Eugen created.

Only eighteen months after her impassioned letter to her first husband, Elinor Wylie died. The lives of the two women had been bound in so many ways—and Edna knew she had to let Bill know that the friendship had been important in all their lives, but Edna kept putting off writing to Bill.

For even though Edna was a prolific poet, she did not relish letter writing. Indeed she once wrote to a professor friend ". . . there is practically nothing under the sun or moon which I would not rather do than write a letter (and in particular begin it; I don't mind it so much after I have really made a start . . . I would rather wash dishes all day; I would rather do a big washing on an old-fashioned scrubbing board; I would rather lay a pipe-line; I would rather dig a grave)."

Finally, twelve days after Elinor's death, Edna went to her desk to celebrate her friendship with Elinor—and to write to Bill.

Steepletop, Austerlitz, N.Y.
December 28, 1928

Dearest Bill,

. . . Yesterday we were in the cellar, sampling the new wine which Pierre our cook has made, and there on a shelf we saw the tiny keg labeled SEVEN SHIRES which we had been keeping for Elinor. It was that wine we had that she liked so much, you remember. We were keeping it for her; nobody was allowed to touch it. When you come here, we will give the little keg to you, and we will all drink to our beautiful, brilliant, adorable one. She is not out of our minds or off our tongue for very long. We talk of her for hours at a time, just as we used to do.

. . . Bill, dear, don't torture yourself with thinking if only you had been better to her. It was you just as you were that she loved, & loved so truly. She was so wise, and though she was often hurt by thoughtless or tactless words not meant to hurt her, I think that a few moments later she understood &

forgave, as she did once with me when I had wounded her deeply without of course wishing to wound her at all. People always torture themselves in this way; I could do it, too, remembering that I hurt her, but instead I remember the happy times. . . .

With so much
love from Eugen
& myself,
Vincent*

*As she was called by family and close friends.

*"Your letter was a great
comfort to me.
I was kind of low...."*

𝓘T WAS A friendship that served both women well. Mabel Dodge and Gertrude Stein met in Paris in 1911, a period when Stein was beset by doubts about her writing and needed the reassurance of someone other than her companion Alice B. Toklas. Mabel Dodge was a collector of people and art, and her acquaintance and subsequent friendship with Stein gave her entrée to many salons and provided her with lively conversation and insights into that remarkable period of creativity that flourished between Paris and New York during the first part of the twentieth century.

The letter reprinted here was sent in response to one from

Mabel to "Dearest Gertrude" sent early in 1912 in which she urged her friend not to be discouraged over her book. As she wrote, "It's *too good* to get immediate attention. Pubs. will be afraid of it at first. If someone would die (& someone may any minute) & leave me a fortune I'd make you let me publish it — I'd *adore* to. I believe it's the biggest thing of our time . . ."

Upon receiving the letter Stein took her cream-colored lightweight paper engraved with 27 RUE DE FLEURUS in bright red ink and in response, using dark blue ink, she wrote:

My dear Mabel.

Your letter was a great comfort to me. I was kind of low in my mind about the publication end and even Wagner's letters were ceasing to be a comfort to me. I have been trying some English publishers with collections of the shorter and longer things those you saw and the ones I did this summer and when I first came back but there is nothing doing. I am working on four books now. One is a long gay book and has lots and lots of everything in it and goes on. It will be quite long. I have written about 120 pages of it. Another is a study of two a man and woman having the same means of xpression and the same emotional and spiritual xperiences with different quality of intellect. That is going very well and slowly.

Then I am doing one that will be finished in a couple of months that consists of many portraits of women. Then I am doing another which is a description of a family of five who are all peculiar and are in a peculiar relation each one to every other one of the five of them. This one is just fairly begun.

I am still sending the volumes of the short and longer things about but they come back, quite promptly and with very polite handwritten and sometimes regretful refusals. The long book is in America. I have not heard anything of it for a long time. You can understand how much I appreciated your letter.

. . . the futurists are in town. You know [Filippo] Marinetti and his crowd. He brought a bunch of painters who paint houses and people and streets and wagons and scaffoldings and bottles and fruits all moving and where they are not moving there are cubes to fill in. They have a catalogue that has a fiery introduction demolishing the old salons and they are xhibiting at Bernheims and everybody goes. Marinetti has given several conferences and at the last he attacked the art of the Greeks and [Elie] Nadelman who was present called him a bad name and Marinetti hit Nadelman and they were separated.

I am afraid we won't see you until the fall. We are going to Spain this year instead of Italy. We leave the first of May and will go slowly down to Granada getting there in July and spending July and August between there and Tangiers. Surely we will meet here in the fall. . . . [Jacques-Emile]

Blanche has been here and I have met him at shows. He is worried to death there is so much doing in funny kinds of art these days. He does not know what bothers him the most. He was almost xhausted entirely by a picture that Picasso calls a portrait of Buffalo Bill . . .

> Much love to you
> always
> Gertrude

"... it takes at least 10 years to realize the death of a parent ..."

$\mathcal{T}$HEY MET THE way two poets should meet—through poetry. Later he was to believe that her poetry unlocked his muse, and so Robert Duncan traced his career as a poet to that time when his California high-school teacher first read H.D.'s poem "Heat" to the class. H.D. (Hilda Doolittle) was a well-known American poet and novelist of the imagist movement, a poetic movement that flourished in both the United States and England between 1909 and 1917. Among the well-known imagists were Ezra Pound and Amy Lowell; imagists placed primary reliance on the use of precise images to express poetry in language within the grasp of readers.

Although H.D. lived primarily in England, she visited New York frequently where she first met Robert Duncan. The two had a lengthy friendship-by-letter, but only thirty-five letters are known to exist today. Still in their work and writing, each fueled the other.

This letter is indicative of the friendship and illustrates not only the imagist style but the depth of feeling that existed between the two poets.

Jan. 12, 1961

Dear Robert,

I haven't written you for a long time now, Jan 2 letter about your mother who "died at the winter solstice." Mine went at spring solstice, in her sleep, but there were all the different distances that you speak of to catch up to or fill in, through the years. I remember how Dr. Hanns Sachs in Vienna said, "it takes at least 10 years to realize the death of a parent." I know, in a way, what he means now. I was in Territet; it suddenly oddly seemed that the *mountains* were or contained my mother who had died in New Jersey. Of course, I *knew* this mountain symbolism, our "return to earth," but I had not *felt* it.

. . . This is an inadequate note to thank you for writing — let me hear again.

"... We are all so close together, Mother, and always will be — life or death."

$\mathcal{O}$NLY A MOTHER who has lost a child knows the kind of grief and suffering that follows.

Anne Morrow Lindbergh, who experienced the heights of love and joy in her life, also faced the shock and numbing disbelief of the kidnapping of her firstborn, Charles A. Lindbergh, Jr., on March 1, 1932, when the child was eighteen months old. For ten weeks the family lived in a state of heightened suspense as the negotiations with the kidnappers continued. And then, after the ransom money was delivered, the dead body of the child was found in the woods a few miles from the family home.

As Anne Morrow Lindbergh wrote, ". . . there is no aristocracy of grief. Grief is a great leveler. There is no highroad out." In her diary she described the difference in grief between a man's feeling for his son and a mother's. "There is something very deep in a man's feeling for his son, it reaches further into the future. My grief is for the small intimate everyday person."

Yet in the midst of her grief Anne Morrow Lindbergh reached out both to her mother and her mother-in-law; both were her dear friends and sources of emotional support. Her letters during that period were filled with her concerns for them as well as for her child.

A month after the baby's body was found, Elizabeth Morrow, Anne's mother, made plans to go to Europe. The night before she left the Lindberghs were with her, and the next day, the grieving Anne (who was pregnant with her second child) wrote a letter of love and friendship to her lifelong companion, her mother.

Englewood, June 15, 1932
Mother darling—

You said last night, just like a little girl: "You're not going to miss me at all!" And I shall miss you terribly. I don't suppose we any of us face what you are to us—I know I don't. I am afraid to realize it, as though, if I did, it would be taken away from me, as though one's only security lay in unconsciousness. A pagan feeling: "If I let 'them' know how much she means, 'they' will be envious."

I can only think of that first week in Hopewell, of you as an ultimate fortress I had, an ultimate source of strength. . . .

. . . I don't know where your ultimate source of strength is, and I feel that I have taken and taken and taken and not given anything back. Perhaps I can't give anything now. It is as though all of us close to this had lost our faith and once it was smashed we were vulnerable—anything could happen. As though your faith, a beautiful shimmering armor of glass, protected you infallibly as long as it was whole. But it's so fragile—once it's gone to pieces you have nothing.

. . . I do feel as though we needed Daddy terribly now. [Anne's father, Dwight Morrow, died the previous year]. I don't think his was ever smashed. It was so wonderful that I can feel it now. I think we all do. We are all so close together,

Mother, and always, always will be—life or death. That is wonderful, and I do honestly believe it.

This is such a sad letter, and goes too far in. But there is so little time to say things. I am always putting away things that are too real to say, and then they never get said. We are always bargaining with our feelings so that we can live from day to day. And you must know—and knew last night—that I love you terribly and humbly and that I'm going to miss you. . . .

*"... no moment must
be lost when a heart
is breaking ..."*

$\mathcal{F}$RIENDSHIP WAS NEVER something to be taken for granted to Emily Dickinson. It was a way of life. As a little girl she wrote impassioned letters detailing her activities and affection to her dearest friends, her classmates. Often she chided them for not responding sooner—Emily considered even a one or two day delay in letter writing to be a breach of friendship etiquette requiring an apology.

The letters she wrote from the time she was fourteen indicate the profound importance of these relationships in her life. There were the school friends, the friends of the family, and just as importantly the friendships formed within her family. Through letter writing she managed to sustain and even increase her circle of friends throughout her life. By the time she was thirty she had determined to confine herself to her home. Yet even though she was not out in the world, she was of the world, and in her remarkable letters she captured and distilled the feelings of all our lives.

Two of her friends were Samuel Bowles and his wife Mary. Samuel Bowles was the son of the founder of the *Springfield Daily Republican,* and Emily Dickinson evidently admired him deeply and also retained a strong tie to his wife; when Emily heard of his death, she immediately communicated with Mary and wrote what she would later call *the broken words:*

To remember our own Mr. Bowles is all we can do.

With grief it is done, so warmly and long, it can never be new.

The couplet was signed "Emily," and Mary Bowles evidently responded directly to Emily.

Later, with time to expand her thoughts more fully, Emily Dickinson wrote this letter of compassion and concern to Mary Bowles.

early 1878

I hasten to you, Mary, because no moment must be lost when a heart is breaking, for though it broke so long, each time is newer than the last, if it broke truly. To be willing that I should speak to you was so generous, dear.

Sorrow almost resents love, it is so inflamed.

I am glad if the broken words helped you. I had not hoped so much, I felt so faint in uttering them, thinking of your great pain. Love makes us "heavenly" without our trying in the least. 'Tis easier than a Saviour—it does not stay on high and call us to its distance; its low "Come unto me" begins in every place. It makes but one mistake, it tells us it is "rest"—perhaps its toil is rest, but what we have not known we shall know again, that divine "again" for which we are all breathless.

I am glad you "work." Work is a bleak redeemer, but it does redeem; it tires the flesh so that can't tease the spirit.

Dear "Mr. Sam" is very near, these midwinter days. When purples come on Pelham, in the afternoon we say "Mr. Bowles's colors." I spoke to him once of his Gem chapter [the reference may be to Revelation 21], and the beautiful eyes rose till they were out of reach of mine, in some hallowed fathom.

> Not that he goes—we love him more
> Who led us while he stayed.
> Beyond earth's trafficking frontier,
> For what he moved, he made.

Mother is timid and feeble, but we keep her with us. She thanks you for remembering her, and never forgets you. . . .

Emily

*"... to a friend that
I am afraid of writing
spontaneously."*

𝒜YN RAND WAS a woman whose passions were never in question. She voiced her beliefs in the best-selling novels, *The Fountainhead* and *Atlas Shrugged*.

The image we have of Ayn Rand comes from tough philosophical stance; her letters, however, reveal a surprisingly softer, yielding side.

She wrote thousands of letters to her parents and sisters whom she left in Russia in 1926 when she came to the United States and—from the time they met—she loved her husband Frank O'Connor.

One of the great friendships of her life was with Isabel

Paterson, whose politics closely resembled Ayn Rand's. Paterson was a columnist for the *New York Herald Tribune* and an author.

But the friendship of Isabel Paterson and Ayn Rand was not to last their lives; it ended in 1948 after Paterson visited the O'Connors in California and, in Rand's words, insulted some of Rand's friends.

But when the friendship was good, it was very, very good and an additional source of strength to two very strong women.

The following letter was written to Isabel Paterson (whom Rand called Pat) following the great success of *The Fountainhead* and evidently was sent after a long period of noncorrespondence. What Rand says about the difficulty of letter writing and the expression of friendship still stands as truth for all of us.

July 26, 1945

Dear Pat,

Thank you!

I have been afraid to write to you—but this time I want so much to thank you that I'm writing. I have received the two bestseller lists you sent me, and now I've received the third one. It means so much to me that I don't know what to say about it. It has knocked me out of equilibrium and made me slightly dizzy, for many reasons: not only the sale of the book itself, but the fact that you're watching it and that you wanted to send the lists to me. Of course I have been thinking all this time that you predicted the sale of the book and that "Isabel Paterson is always right." I wanted to gloat over it with you. I'm doing the gloating here in your honor anyway—but I wanted to tell you about it, so I'm writing.

I'm not sure that you won't give me hell for saying that I was afraid to write to you—and that you'll be offended by it. I can only say that of all the things I can do in relation to you, the one I *don't* want to do, above all else, is to offend you or to hurt you in any way whatever. I was at fault originally, that time when I didn't write to you for over a month. But when I tried to write and explain it, I made it worse. When I received your last letter, I wrote you six pages—and didn't send them. I thought anything I say will make it worse again. Because, you see, I never thought that I wrote letters as a "favor" *for* a friend. I always thought that I wrote primarily for my own sake, because I wanted to talk to a friend and wanted to hear from the friend. Assuming at the same time, of course, that the friend did want to hear from me. But I never thought of it as being a matter of an "Ungenerous heart" on my part. So that if I suffer writing letters, I am a martyr for my own sake—not anyone else's, nor am I doing it only because the friend will get mad if I don't, nor am I saying I am tired as a reproach, that is, to show in effect: look how much I am sacrificing for you. This is what you read into my last letter. It is

not what I intended. So that gave me another good complex about letter writing—sheer terror of the mere attempt.

I know the reason why letters are so hard for me to write—and I will tell it to you, not as alibiing, but because it is a fact. Don't say in answer, "My good woman, if it's terror to you don't have to write to me." The point is that I *do* want to write to you—but that I cannot do it easily,—but there is a valid reason for my complex. It's this: the first letters I ever wrote regularly were to my family in Russia, when I came here—and every letter was censored, so I had to be extremely careful of what I said, in order not to embarrass them. I always rewrote page after page, before I could mail a letter to them. I had to doubt and scrutinize every sentence for any possible misinterpretation. I have not been able to write any kind of letter spontaneously ever since.

I am very consciously aware of the fact that words on paper can be taken in very many different ways. So I am always trying to write letters as if I were walking on thin ice—so that what I say would be taken the way I said it. And, above all, it is letters to friends that I compose the most carefully—because that is when I want to be understood, and the things I write about are important. You said, "I assume that one speaks to a friend or writes a letter, spontaneously." I speak to a friend spontaneously—yes. But it is precisely to a friend that I am afraid of writing spontaneously. In conversation, a misunderstanding can be sensed and corrected at once. On paper—it's done. I had always gone over all my long letters to you, and edited them very carefully, and rewrote them. The sad part of it all is that my last letter to you was the first one I sent unedited and uncopied. And it was the one that did offend you. I am not saying this as a reproach to you. I can see your point and why you could take it as you did. It only made me realize more concretely my limitations as a letter-writer.

All I can say now is that I want to try and write to you. BECAUSE I WANT TO WRITE TO YOU. I hope you will also want to hear. But the effort is made for my sake, not as a bribe to you. I had hoped to be in New York much sooner and speak to you in person, rather than try to say anything on paper. . . .

Now, as to my personal life, I haven't much of it. Haven't the time nor the energy. I love living in the country, and I get furiously nervous every time I have to go out and meet somebody. I am becoming more anti-social than I was—and the reason is the same as yours, so I think you'll understand very well: I can't stand the sort of things people talk about. I've stopped reading the newspapers, beyond a general glance at the news. I can't stand the columnists and editorials: what they're doing in the world now is beyond any polite discussion and beyond the possibility of a legitimate disagreement between decent people . . .

My happiest thoughts are, of course, about *The Fountainhead*. You know how I'd feel about the sale. It's gone much beyond what I expected. You remember I set myself 100,000 copies as the goal at which I'd be satisfied. It has sold 150,000 or more by now. I like to think that it might be a sign that there are many more people sick of collectivism than I expected. . . .

I had started this as a short note to you—but there's so much that I'd like to talk to you about. I still don't know whether you want me to write in detail, and I feel a little presumptuous doing this. I just want to say one more thing: if you wonder how I feel about you, look at what I wrote in your copy of *The Fountainhead*. I meant it. I still do. I always will.

> Love from both of
> us—Frank wants
> his included
> specifically . . .

*"If one could only
rid one's mind, completely
of <u>words</u> during the night,
one would be better."*

$\mathcal{S}$HE WAS WONDERFULLY wacky—and so was her family, the fabled Sitwells. English-born, Dame Edith and her brothers Osbert and Sacheverell were *the* literary family of England in the first part of the twentieth century.

Dame Edith Sitwell, as noted for her eccentric behavior and dramatic dress as for her poetry and biographies, would have been a darling of our modern tabloid press. Today's popular magazines would have loved to chronicle her escapades had she been born thirty years later!

Her writing had a rhythm all its own—and so did her

friendships. In her writing she disdained pretensions, and one must assume that even her friendships were stripped of the usual clichés. No dreary little "so sorry" and "I feel for you" were ever in evidence. Instead, one has the sense of her brushing aside pretext and convention and asking the rest of the world to do the same.

This letter was sent to Lady Snow (Pamela Hansford Johnson), the wife of Sir Charles Snow. Lady Snow, a writer of some repute, had evidently written a letter complaining of her minor physical ills to Dame Edith, and Dame Edith, instead of responding with the expected or standard expressions of sympathy, responded in her own singular fashion—a letter so filled with sizzle, snap, and humor that it was sure to lift anyone out of the doldrums.

My dear Pamela,

Thank you so much for your letter.

I am so distressed to hear you have insomnia. It is horrible, and one really suffers greatly. When I am in London, sometimes I only sleep for two hours a night, if that.

If one could only rid one's mind, completely of *words* during the night, one would be better.

It hasn't worked lately, because I have been too tired to sleep, anyhow, but at one moment, the following would send me to sleep—and strangely enough, Osbert had the same habit—to imagine oneself in a gondola floating through Venice and regarding, under a full moon—with no sound excepting that of an oar, and nothing near one—only the sleeping palaces, as one floated on and on.

On a more mundane note, a tumbler of *hot* beer in bed can work—or indeed, cold, if it comes to that.

Those tireless nuisances the Income Tax people have written to ask me where I was last employed, and if I gave satisfaction, and when, if at all, I left it.

So I am going to reply that I was last employed, in a menial capacity, by Miss Imregarde A. Potter, of 8 The Grove, Leamington Spa, in 1911; but that I did not give satisfaction: there was some small unpleasantness, and I was dismissed without a character. And that if they want any more details, will they write to Dan Macmillan (whose temper, as you and Charles will know, needs a little sugar adding). Oh, good gracious!

My love and admiration to you both,

Yours affectionately,
Edith

And my love to the
Poet [their son], too

"... we must go now,
I to die, you to live."

$\mathcal{I}$F SHARED SECRETS and shared tragedies are the currency of friendship, then Hannah Arendt and Mary McCarthy were wealthy women. They traded information and advice in their letters, but most importantly they served as the kind of confidantes that only those who share a talent can understand.

Hannah Arendt worried often about the health of her husband, Heinrich Blucher, and Mary McCarthy, who had worries of her own, listened always with a loving heart.

And then, suddenly, Hannah Arendt's beloved husband died of a heart attack the first week in November 1970. The only reason that Mary was not among Hannah's friends who immediately assembled at the couple's New York apartment was that Mary and her husband, James West, were in Paris. So they telephoned Hannah and then wrote.

A memorial service for Heinrich Blucher was held within days of his death, and a few weeks later another service was conducted at Bard College. Mary McCarthy urged her friend to tell her about the Bard service, and so Hannah Arendt did.

But she did something more. With the kind of candor only close, nonjudgmental friends are free to employ, Hannah Arendt told her loving friend Mary McCarthy openly and honestly how she felt during those terrible first weeks after her husband's death.

New York
Sunday, 11/22/70

Dearest Mary,

. . . Your cards and letters—so dear and then also so immensely sensible, just the day-to-day continuity of life and friendship.

The Bard ceremony. Very decent, especially Shafer [Frederick Shafer was Professor of Philosophy and Religion at Bard] who read from the *Apology,* Socrates's words about death, concluding with the great last sentence—we must go now, I to die, you to live. Which is better is known to the god alone. Such decency, and rightness. And from a clergyman. The cemetery is a piece of woods with markers here and there not even real graves. Very good, very right.

After that, the very next day, back to school. I was very frightened, gave a very good seminar and, on Thursday, the lecture course all right. Am not at all sure if I should not be ashamed of myself. The truth is that I am completely exhausted if you understand by that no superlative of tiredness. I am not tired, or not much tired, just exhausted. I function all right but know that the slightest mishap could throw me off balance. I don't think I told you that for ten long years I had been constantly afraid that just such a sudden death would happen. This fear frequently bordered on real panic. Where the fear was and the panic there is now sheer emptiness. Sometimes I think without this heaviness inside me I can no longer walk. And it is true. I feel like floating. If I think even a couple of months ahead I get dizzy.

I am sitting now in Heinrich's room and using his typewriter. Gives me something to hold on to. The weird thing is that at no moment am I actually out of control. Perhaps this is a process of petrification. Perhaps not. Don't know . . .

Mountains of mail, among them students' letters—some very good, very touching. In Bard, William Lansing, the chairman of the philosophy department who had always been his [Heinrich's] enemy. Sobbing, out of control, how terrible the last semesters had been without Heinrich. He is the hunter there and the "love" of firearms or bow and arrows

124

had been the bridge between them. So I gave him Heinrich's rifle . . .

In the mountains of letters: from my whole past, layer upon layer, none conventional, with sympathy or old friendship still alive. Strange. . . .

De tout coeur
Hannah

*"You may say
I long for death . . .
but I long even more
to be cured."*

$\mathcal{S}$HE NEVER WROTE an autobiography, but she did write eight thousand letters. That feat alone would have made her one of the great letter writers of the twentieth century, but what truly made her a memorable correspondent was her wit, her comments on outrageous gossip, and the distinguished friends with whom her letters were exchanged—among them Evelyn Waugh, Harold Acton, Robert Byron, Cyril Connolly, and Raymond Mortimer.

Nancy Mitford was born in 1904 into an English family best-known for the talents of seven lively children including Jessica, the writer, and Unity, whose friendship with Hitler was a cause for great comment in the 1930s and 1940s. In 1946, after a marriage and career as a writer in England, Nancy Mitford moved to France where she lived for the rest of her life.

Even as a child she considered letter writing important, so important that she carefully chose her writing paper. In childhood there were small sheets with her nickname "Nance" printed in gold against a colored oval. If she wrote on plain paper, she apologized. Most of her letters were written in the morning as she sat up in bed, and she always ended a letter at the bottom of a page.

Evidences of her wit are in all her letters, but nowhere is the wit more trenchant than in this letter to her longtime friend, the writer Raymond Mortimer, as she writes to tell him that she plans to go to England for treatment but doubts that she will be able to see him.

10 October 1970
4 rue d'Artois
Versailles

Darling Raymond

English doctors have killed 3/4 of my friends & the joke is the remaining 1/4 go on recommending them, so odd is human nature. We have seen the same thing with Louis XIV & Fagon [Guy Crescent Fagon, Louis XIV's doctor, whom Nancy described as a "killer of Princes" in *Madame de Pompadour*]. You may say I long for death well, yes, but I long even more to be cured. Dr. Selmes hasn't killed anybody known to me & has cured 3 so I don't mind trying him. If he doesn't do, Grace Dudley will take me to Munich—then Monica Stirling will take me to Lausanne. My good doctor here says *il faut rapper a toutes les portes.* I shall get to know Europe. I haven't been to England for three years & had hoped never to go again.

I will telephone if I can . . . The Dr will only know when he sees me—but I understand he may do something & send me home for a month or . . . put me in Guildford . . . or keep me in London for treatment for a week or two.

The pain is worse than any I have had which is saying a good deal & I wonder how I can endure the journey . . .

I've always felt the great importance of getting into the right set at once on arrival in Heaven. I used to think the Holland House lot would suit me—now I'm not sure. One would get some good belly laughs no doubt, but Sans Souci might provide more nourishment. The Paris salons are all under the thumb of tiresome, jealous ladies. . . . The thing is, one must be careful in a new place not to get into uncongenial company. Let's make for the same objective—what do you think? I wonder what Louise [a friend who died the previous year] is doing about it.

. . . There I've bored you for long enough.

Much love
et j'espere a bientot
N

IV

The Ties that Bind

the perfect marriage

Someone asked me to name the time
Our friendship ended
And love began.
Oh, my darling, that's the secret.
Our friendship never ended.

"... I received a Letter from
my Friend ... it was a cordial
to my Heart."

O F ALL THE tender friendships women have, none is more rare or more perfect than when that friendship exists between a woman and her husband.

Perhaps the most celebrated of all such friendships was that between Abigail and John Adams, whose life together was marked by many separations, and each separation was punctuated by their letters in which each professed not only love but undying friendship.

The reason that Abigail, an eighteenth-century American, was able to read and write at a time when daughters were "wholly neglected in point of Literature," is that her father was a parson. Like many young women who grew up in the parsonage, Abigail had books available to her and was able to meet well-read people in her own parlor.

For more than fifty years John and Abigail maintained a remarkable, supportive relationship kept fresh during separations by their letters. From their hundreds of letters it is possible to find in each missive at least a few words that express deep friendship and trust. This letter was written when Abigail was pregnant; her baby is due momentarily, and she confesses her fears and concerns to her husband. With a woman's prescience she seems to prepare him for an unhappy ending.

Two days after this letter was written, Abigail was delivered of a stillborn daughter.

July 10 (1777) 9 o'clock Evening

About an Hour ago I received a Letter from my Friend dated June 21: beginning in this manner "my dearest Friend." It gave me a most agreable Sensation, it was a cordial to my Heart. That one single expression dwelt upon my mind and playd about my Heart, and was more valuable to me than any part of the Letter, except the close of it. It was because my Heart was softned and my mind enervated by my sufferings, and I wanted the personal and tender soothings of my dearest Friend, that [ren]derd it so valuable to me at this time. I have [no] doubt of the tenderest affection or sincerest regard of my absent Friend, yet an expression of that kind will sooth my Heart to rest amidst a thousand anxietyes.

Tis now 48 Hours since I can say I really enjoyed any Ease, nor am I ill enough to summons any attendance unless my sisters. Slow, lingering and troublesome is the present situation. The Dr. encourages me to Hope that my apprehensions are groundless respecting what I wrote you yesterday, tho I cannot say I have had any reason to allter my mind. My spirits However are better than they were yesterday, and I almost wish I had not let that Letter go. If there should be agreable News to tell you, you shall know it as soon as the post can convey it. I pray Heaven that it may be soon or it seems to me I shall be worn out. I must lay my pen down at this moment, to bear what I cannot fly from—and now I have endured it I reassume my pen and will lay by all my own feelings and thank you for your obligeing Letters. . . . We have the finest Season here that I have known for many years. The fruit was injured by the cold East winds and falls of, the Corn looks well, Hay will be plenty, but your Farm wants manure. I shall endeavour to have Sea weed carted every Leasure moment that can be had. That will not be many. Help is so scarce and so expensive I can not Hire a days mowing under 6 shillings.

Howe has done himself no honour by his late retreat. We fear most now for Tycon[deroga]. Tis reported to day that tis taken. We have a vast many men who look like officers continually riding about. I wonder what they can be after, why they do not repair to the army.

We wonder too what Congress are a doing? We have not heard of late.

How do you do? Are you glad you are out of the way of sour faces. I could look pleasent upon you in the midst of sufferings—allmighty God carry me safely through them. There I would hope I have a Friend ever night and ready to assist me, unto whom I commit myself.

This is Thursday Evening. It cannot go till monday, and then I hope will be accompanied with more agreable inteligance.

Most sincerely
Yours.

"I just wanted you to know
I am thinking of you and
wish I lived nearer."

In THE BEGINNING Elizabeth Bishop may have written letters to help overcome her innate shyness and communicate more openly with others. In time her letters became a record of her life; she wrote thousands of letters to friends, letters filled with love, anger, intrigues. Like most who can love deeply, she could be hurt, angry, and unforgiving. Among her correspondents were some of the greatest writers of the twentieth century: Robert Lowell, James Merrill, Richard Wilbur, Mary McCarthy, Edmund Wilson — and the list goes on.

The letter to Marianne Moore shows Elizabeth Bishop's humor, her generosity, her interest in others and, as in so many of the letters she wrote, some reflection about her current reading. Her correspondence with Marianne Moore began in 1934 and is one of the more important exchanges in the lives of both poets.

October 10, 1968

I had a letter from Louise this morning & she told me you had been in Lenox Hill for about ten days. . . . I am so sorry I didn't know about this sooner; it is really my own fault because I haven't written to Anny the way I should. Louise says that you are well now, however, and at home again, and I do hope you are feeling better for your stay. I didn't mind Lenox Hill too much when I stayed there; it seemed very good for a *hospital*. And if one has Anny to defend one, one gets along very well. (I did balk at having a TV, however, and had it returned behind her back!)

I didn't tell you in my postcard that the other day I was in the Supermarket (I love to go there to read the packages, it is just like a library, really) and I saw a number of *Family Circle* with "Marianne Moore on Baseball" on the cover & of course I bought it. May Sarton, Truman Capote are also in this number. I think it must be getting to be the fashionable publication. I haven't any news, really. I am about two-thirds through the Wallace Stevens *Letters* and find them much more fascinating than I'd thought they'd be. He must have been a bit of a disciplinarian, though. I liked his saying that when he came home from the office the first thing he did was make people take things off the tops of his radiators. He enjoys everything so much, too, and I also like his preoccupation with the weather and climates.

One poet I've met here, almost a neighbor, I like very much, Thom Gunn. His poetry is usually very good, I think; he's English but has lived here for a long time. I am going to Harvard sometime at the end of this month—I'm afraid I won't be able to get to New York, however . . . But I'm coming back next May to give those readings . . .

I just wanted you to know I am thinking of you and wish I lived nearer. If there's anything I can send you from California—I can't seem to think of anything at the moment except maybe those crystallized fruits (do you like them?)—please please let me know. I'm rather disappointed in the California fruits & vegetables so far. I made lemon jelly and it had no taste of lemon. . . .

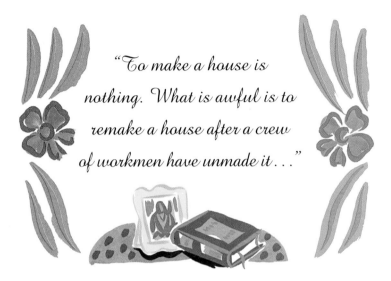

"To make a house is nothing. What is awful is to remake a house after a crew of workmen have unmade it..."

$\mathcal{C}$OLETTE WAS NOT only a storyteller, she was a life force whose own story—a first husband who forced her to write, a mother she adored, a daughter she cherished and, finally, a husband who loved her as she loved him—reads like fiction. In addition to her huge literary output, Colette was an energetic, effusive letter writer. According to her third husband, Maurice Goudeket, she averaged a half-dozen letters daily. In contrast to her carefully edited stories, she wrote with abandon letters covering her daily activities which could range from truffle gathering to ski lessons.

Many letters were written to Marguerite Moreno, an actress who began her career with the *Comédie Française* and later made films. She has been described as Colette's greatest friend, so it is no surprise that the frustrations as well as the pleasures of daily life were shared with her.

This series of letters depicts a time of frustration. As anyone who has ever built, remodeled, or dealt in any way with workmen knows, there's the feeling of imminent disaster when a house is incomplete and the whole world looks unfinished.

What is needed is a friend, a friend who'll listen and lend a reassuring shoulder and who promises it will all turn out fine.

Colette, in 1928, upon finding her house in Saint-Tropez unexpectedly incomplete, dashed off a letter to Marguerite. As the household settled, however, Colette's heart and mind returned to the real centers of her life.

Saint Tropez, July 12, 1928

Ah! my Marguerite! What a week! I haven't written you because I didn't want to bore you—and also, my Lord, because there wouldn't have been any place to write except my knees. We arrived (though a last minute telegram, advising me to postpone coming for a fortnight, had sobered me) to find an indescribable house, with all the furniture of the principal room emptied into the two others, one of these being the bathroom. No sheets on any of the beds. The stove moved out into the garage, blocking the place for the car, and in this same garage, Louise in tears, trying to grill a fish on a tiny petrol stove. . . . My dear, you can't believe what I found—due to the workmen's failure to keep their promise. The WC's which were to have been moved had simply disappeared, and their replacements were, if I may say so, not yet *enclosed*. Nothing done—you understand? Nothing! . . .

I passed a foul night. The next morning I called in the boss, and then, in four hellish days, I organized three weeks' work. But if I leave now, everything is lost. You understand. I'm staying put—and our visit will have to be postponed to September. My poor little daughter is charming. She is painting all the roof beams and jargonizing with the Italian workers . . .

July 22

It's turned warm here, but my daughter and I haven't had time to pay attention. To make a house is nothing. What is awful is to remake a house after a crew of workmen have unmade it . . .

After the first ten days, the workers themselves have admitted that they have never gotten so much done, and the so-called North Court is a marvel of simplicity and balance. Maurice arrived yesterday and couldn't believe his eyes. . . .

143

August

My daughter left yesterday, black and burnt rose, bursting in her skin, altogether gentle and sweet with her mother, but I glimpsed all the demons of despotism, foxtrotting, fast cars and gramophones which she is about to let loose on the three teenage boys at Germaine's. . . .

Maurice has been here since last Saturday—one week. He savors the heat, the sea, and my patio court (which is charming) with a mostly silent passion—always the perfect companion, warm, full of tact, and born under the sign of Apropos.

Phelps, Robert, ed. Letters from Colette.
New York: Farrar, Straus and Giroux, Inc., 1980.

*"... you and my own sister
are the three women who are
tied to my heart by a cord which
can never be broken ..."*

$\mathcal{N}$OTHING TESTS FEMALE friendship like a woman's passionate relationship with a man. And should a woman's love cause her to flout society's mores—and, even worse, should she confide in her men friends before confiding in her women friends—that would put the greatest strain of all on the relationship between the women.

So when the news that the unmarried George Eliot (the pseudonym of Marian Evans) chose to live with her married lover, George Henry Lewes, Marian's best friends felt betrayed and unhappy because, before telling them, she'd told her men friends.

Marian's friends were angry, and they let her know by means of a reproachful letter.

Upon receiving it, Marian immediately wrote an impassioned letter to her dear friends, Sarah Hennell and Cara Bray, reassuring them of the importance of their friendship to her.

Marian Evans did what every woman tries to do when a crisis in friendship arises—she sought to recover the good will and to repair the bond that ties friend to friend.

31 October, 1854

My dear Sarah,

The mode in which you and Cara have interpreted both my words and my silence makes me dread lest in writing more I should only give rise to fresh misconceptions. I am so deeply conscious of having had neither the feeling nor the want of feeling which you impute to me that I am quite unable to read into my words, quoted by you, the sense which you put upon them. When you say that I do not care about Cara's or your opinion and friendship it seems much the same to me as if you said that I didn't care to eat when I was hungry or to drink when I was thirsty. One of two things: either

I am a creature without affection, on whom the memories of years have no hold, or, you, Cara and Mr. Bray (Cara's husband) are the most cherished friends I have in the world. It is simply self-contradictory to say that a person can be indifferent about her dearest friends; yet this is what you substantially say, when you accuse me of 'boasting with what serenity I can give you up,' of 'speaking proudly' etc. The only reply I can give to such an accusation is an absolute denial that I have been actuated by such a spirit as you describe with regard to any one thing which I have written, done, or left undone.

You say: 'You' shew that 'you wish to have communication with Charles only.' The reason why I wrote to Mr. Bray and not to you and Cara is simply this. Before I left England, I communicated, by Mr. Lewes's desire, certain facts in strict confidence to Mr. Bray and Mr. Chapman [an editor] and I did so for special reasons which would not apply to any female friend. After your kind letters came to me, we heard much painful news from London as to reports which were partly a perversion of the truth, partly pure falsehood. I cannot, even now, see that I did anything deserving so severe a reproach as you send me, in writing to Mr. Bray who was already in possession of the main facts, and in intimating that my silence to you arose from no want of affection, but from what I, falsely perhaps, but still sincerely, regarded as the very reverse of *pride* and a spirit of *boasting*.

There is no longer any secrecy to be preserved about Mr. Lewes's affairs or mine, and what I have written to Mr. Bray,

I have written to you. I am under no foolish hallucinations about either the present or the future and am standing on no stilts of any kind. I wish to speak simply and to act simply but I think it can hardly be unintelligible to you that I shrink from writing elaborately about private feelings and circumstances. I have really felt it a privation that I have been unable to write you about things not personal, in which I know you would feel a common interest, and it will brighten my thoughts very much to know that I may do so. Cara, you and my own sister are the three women who are tied to my heart by a cord which can never be broken and which really *pulls* me continually. My love for you rests on a past which no future can reverse, and offensive as the words seem to have been to you, I must repeat, that I can feel no bitterness towards you, however you may act towards me. If you remain to me what you have ever been, my life will be all the happier, and I will try not to be unworthy of your love so far as faithfulness to my own conscience can make me worthy of it.

I have written miserably ill, and I fear all the while that I am writing that I may be giving rise to some mistake. But interpret my whole letter so as to make it accord with this plain statement — I love Cara and you with unchanged and unchangeable affection, and while I retain your friendship, I retain the best that life has given me next to that which is the deepest and gravest joy in all human experience.

Marian Evans

"Much love to David
& a world of love to you
Maude dear."

ELEANOR ROOSEVELT NEVER played the role of old-fashioned "woman behind the man"; she eschewed the role of America's Number One Housewife, and was always out front with her causes.

She was also always up-front with her friends.

Her friends numbered among the most famous people of her time. Her friends also included members of her family with whom she kept in touch by letter.

Eleanor lectured; she wrote; she gave voice to her worldly concerns.

And late at night, after the meetings and the disappointments and the problems of the day, she wrote to those who mattered most in her life.

Maude Gray, the youngest of Eleanor's aunts, was married to the U.S. Minister to Ireland, and when Eleanor wrote to her in February 1942, it was out of loneliness and love — two qualities her detractors never thought she possessed.

I owe you & David so many apologies. I don't know where to begin so I better just say that I've worked so hard for many months that I've been neglectful of everything else.

First, thanks for all your dear letters & cables & F.D.R. tells me every now & then what a grand job David is doing & that means you, too, Maude dear, for no one can do a diplomatic job alone.

Now for all the family news . . .

Last time I saw Cousin Henry & Susie I did them more harm than good because I was undergoing one of Pegler's* attacks & they were troubled. Both have been far from well this winter . . .

* Westbrook Pegler was a syndicated newspaper columnist who regularly attacked Mrs. Roosevelt as well as the President and their children.

F.D.R. is grand. Stands up even under Singapore without a ripple in his serenity! Churchill's visit was interesting & he is a pleasant guest & a wonderful war leader but I don't want him to make the peace. I gave him Adamic's "Two Way Passage" to help him understand the U.S. I'm sending you a copy, too. I've had so little time to read I've not even read the book you sent me yet but now that I am getting out of the Civilian Defense Office I will have time to breathe again. Since Sept. I've worked all day at the office & every night on mail till 2 or 3 A.M.! It has agreed with me, however!

Elliott is now a navigator on a bomber. Based at Lake Muroc in the Mojave desert & patrolling the Pacific but apt to leave soon for parts unknown. James is back in the active Marine Corps training with a "commando" regiment & expecting to shove off the end of March. Fjr. has seen some hard trips in the North Atlantic but before that had an easy convoy trip to Capetown, S.A. Just now he's recovering well from an appendix removal in the Brooklyn Hospital. I'm so thankful it could be done ashore. I saw him last Sat. & Sunday & go up tonight to see him again tomorrow but I'll be back Friday A.M. as it is my last day at the office. The new babies [Ethel's & Ruth's] both boys are very cunning and healthy.

We are working very slowly to "all out" war but it will come.

Much love to David & a world of love to you Maude dear.

Devotedly always
Eleanor

P.S. I wish you were home so often. I'd give anything to have you here now! I think the N.Y. houses are sold & I've found an apt. on Washington Sq. we can all use.

"... You ask if I really thought I could live in the house with two men who were in love with me...."

*M*AYBE IT WAS the times; maybe it would have happened even if this hadn't been the 1930s, even if M. F. K. (Mary Frances) Fisher had not been as ingenious as she was, even if her husband Al Fisher hadn't agreed, even if their friend Dillwyn (Timmy) Parrish had not thought all three living together in Switzerland was an enchanting idea—but it did happen, and that year in the house above Vevey changed all their lives.

At the end of the year Al accepted a teaching position at Smith College; Mary Frances returned to California and announced that she was going to divorce Al and marry Timmy.

To her dear friend Lawrence Powell, Mary Frances confided the details of her marriage in 1938 probably because she knew that a loving and understanding man could be as good a friend as a loving, understanding woman. And obviously he was a man she trusted. Powell apprenticed at Jake Zeitlin's bookstore in California and later became an authoritative writer on Southwest literature, a critic, a novelist, and eventually chief librarian at UCLA.

Although Mary Frances was to live more than fifty years after her marriage, her time with Timmy was short. He suffered from Buerger's disease, a painful and disabling illness that caused him to take his own life in 1941.

But in 1938 there was the thought only that she must explain herself to her dearest friend—and so she wrote.

2.xii.38
Hotel Huldi
Adelboden

Dearest Larry—

. . . You ask if I really thought I could live in the house with two men who were in love with me. . . . It probably seems as strange to you as it does to me, now. but for so long I had throttled all my sexual needs (it took me a long time to get used to living side by side with a man whom I still loved passionately and who was almost actively sickened at the thought of being with me) that I was pretty sure they were well in control and I had proved that I could be with Tim without setting off any bonfires. So, as far as that part of life went, I truly hadn't a qualm. It was certainty that Al would be bored that worried me — but when I talked about it, he would always assure me that the only thing he really wanted in the world was complete solitude, time to *think*.

As for my leaving Al for Tim, it is quite untrue. I have told Al that, and I think he knows it, but no man likes to admit that a woman has left him for any other reason than another man. . . . I would never have left Al for him. I am sorry that Al won't admit that.

Yes, I've gone ahead with the divorce. It will be granted some time in January, probably. It is very unpleasant to me to be the theoretical wife of a man who has not even seen me for over a year — it's distasteful and dishonest to me at least, and I should think would be to Al, too. I can't understand his wanting things to stay that way — except that being legally married is a kind of protection to him, perhaps.

. . . Al is a master of implication. He can (and does) imply the thousand affairs of a rather pedagogic Don Juan.

But what are they? They are wish-dreams, almost all of them. Al was twenty-six or twenty-seven when he married me, and still a virgin. He was, and still is, frightened and repelled by the actual physical act of love. Even at his freest and happiest, he had to condone it and make it acceptable by quoting what Plato, and Bertrand Russell, and Marie Stopes said about it.

... I hoped desperately that his getting away from me would help him. But I don't think it has. Teaching in a girls' school, always having to be circumspect and cautious, certainly doesn't help. . . .

I hope, and very very much, that some day he will allow himself to be loose and easy and free with me. I rather doubt it, though. . . .

Well, dearest Larry—I remember the first time I ever met you, at a dance at Orr Hall, I said that you had something of the father-confessor in you. Certainly I've proved it today—and for the first time, as far as all this goes. I was too unhappy and sad to talk to *anyone* when I was home. And, of course, I am quite alone with Tim, who knows most of this from having been so close to both Al and me. Let it stay in the confessional, and think no ill of any of us . . .

"... Now I'll tell you
what to do ..."

𝒫EG BRACKEN BECAME an adult during the rosy post-war years of blissful domesticity, a time when, with pasted-on smiles and clenched teeth, women the country over looked up from their hot stoves and assured one another, "I love to cook."

But Peg Bracken, along with Erma Bombeck, knew that despite the serious dishpan hands and rings around the collar, women were just waiting to have their funnybones tickled by a couple of writers who could write about domestic responsibilities with a smile.

Peg started the laughter in the kitchen with *The I Hate to Cook Book*, which promptly became a national bestseller.

Only her best friends knew that outside the slick covers of "that book," the cookbook humorist was a darned good cook.

One of the friends who was in on the secret of the real Peg was Betty Rollin. A writer herself, Betty and Peg met in 1978 when Betty went to Hawaii to give a talk and, at a dinner party, was totally taken with one of the guests she'd never met before, Peg Bracken. Soon the two women found themselves in what both would remember as intimate conversation. Betty mused, "It's surprising that we women can often meet someone and in five minutes find ourselves on the same wavelength and feel comfortable talking about practically anything. Men don't do that as fast as we do — that is, if they ever do it. But what I remember about Peg was that not only was she utterly real, utterly down-to-earth and I felt comfortable with her — what I truly remember is that we connected with humor. Now that doesn't happen often between women. And I liked, too, the fact that we were both married to men named Edwards so we were both Mrs. Edwards."

When Betty came back to New York, she began writing to Peg because, as Betty recalls, "in those days you didn't spend the money to call Hawaii." Yet even after Peg was widowed, remarried, and living in Portland, the two friends continued writing. "I suppose we could call each other now," Betty said, "but we had fallen into the habit of writing. And it's such a nice habit, isn't it? Why give it up?"

Nowadays Peg's letters often contain sketches; always they are filled with her funny view of life. And even more often there is tucked into the envelope, along with the good humor, a good word about food and a way to prepare it.

Betty Rollin, author of several best-selling books herself, confesses that she hasn't saved many letters. The exception is the collection of letters she has received from Peg Bracken, of which this is one.

March 26 or thereabouts

Dear Betty,

Let's see. I have started this letter five times, and each time I got sidetracked into seeing if this word processor would transfer Paragraph 3 on Page 2 to an inviting little space two-thirds of the way down Page 1, or seeing if I could change every "the" in it to an "a," or playing other intriguing games of this nature till it seemed wiser to begin again, and then the same thing would happen. But now I have sworn to bring Nellie into the barn. I am going to go straight.

Do you have one of these little mothers? I had sworn (I swear a lot) I wouldn't be caught dead with a Word Processor. But as I believe I remarked in *Window* and probably some other places, whenever you swear you won't do something, that's what you find yourself doing. *Precisely* what you find yourself doing.

. . . I've been wanting to tell you how much I enjoyed you

and Larry King, and naturally, being a devout fan of you both. What happened was I heard—in the middle of the night via the cord I use that enables me to listen to the radio without waking Parker—that you were going to be interviewed by Larry sometime during the coming week. Then I discovered that we don't get any of Larry's interviews at all during the week, only his "Open Phone America." I was crushed and thought of moving to somewhere civilized. And then I learned that on weekend early ayems we always get "The Best of Larry King," and there you were, and it was such fun, lying there in the soft dark Hawaiian night, listening to you and you sounding lively and lovely and even as though you were having a good time. Were you? Is he as good at his job as he seems to be? Did it sell a lot of books or can't you tell yet?

. . . Now I'll tell you what to do with all this nice spring asparagus that's around in case you were wondering. You peel the claws off it and break each stalk at the tender just-breakable point opposite the blossom end. Then you immerse it in ice-water with lots of ice cubes in it—really freezing cold water—for say ten minutes. Have a pot of water heating at the same time and when it comes to a full rolling boil, drop the A into it. Let it remain till the water comes to a full rolling boil once again, remove the A immediately, drain it quickly, plunge it again into the ice-water to which you've added more ice and let it get freezing cold again. Then drain it on paper towels, dry it gently with same, lay it out on a plate or a platter, cover snugly with Saran Wrap and keep it in the fridge, all day if you like, or till dinner time. You may find, as I did, that it likes to be sung to in the final stages. I recommend a fast chorus of *Funiculi Funicula* during the final (or drying) stage. And I almost forgot—a lot of lemon juice whipped into mayonnaise is a nice sauce for it.

What this does, as you will find out, is produce the most gorgeous just-tender emerald green asparagus you ever et.

And that is about all I know, except that Parker is well and so am I, and the weather is beautiful, and I'm about to go out and get me a *San Francisco Chronicle* to have with Sunday morning breakfast. It is $2.75 here which, for the quality of the paper, is horrendous, but sometimes I get this craving for Herb Caen.

Hope you're having fun and that all is well . . .

Love,

Peg

*"I wish I was this letter,
so I could go in a plane
and be with you quick ."*

$\mathcal{S}$ARA AND GERALD Murphy were the quintessential twenties couple. F. Scott Fitzgerald based many of his characters on them and their famous friends, who included Archibald MacLeish, John Dos Passos, himself and his wife Zelda Fitzgerald, and Ernest Hemingway. All of them, with or without current spouses, visited regularly at the Murphy residences everywhere from New York and East Hampton (where both the families of Sara and Gerald had homes and where the couple first met) to Paris and Cap d'Antibes. In all their time in both Europe and America, it was the habit of the Murphys and their friends to spend as much time together as possible—and when apart to bemoan the fates that separated them. Their longing for one another could be both poignant and humorous.

Dorothy Parker visited the Murphys in Switzerland for a long period in the early 1930s, and when she returned to New York she met the handsome actor-writer Alan Campbell. In June 1934, Campbell and Parker crossed the country by car to go to Hollywood. By the time they got to Raton, a town in New Mexico, they married, and in September were ensconced in a rented house on North Canon Drive in Hollywood and immediately lionized as the highly paid ($1,000 per week) husband and wife writing team of Paramount Pictures.

Did this celebrity and adulation go to Parker's head? As this letter to her dear friends, the Murphys, demonstrates, Ms. Parker never lost her satirical New York edge as she traveled that bumpy road to Hollywood. And she also never lost sight of the fact that no matter how pretty Hollywood was, she still missed her friends.

Beverly Hills (c. January 1935)

Dear Sara and Gerald Murphy,

I am a little girl of 56, and this is my first fan letter. I have admired you ever since I first saw you, and you do not know how happy it would make me to have your autographs on a letter.

I live in a big white house with tall columns and magnolia trees, so that I often feel like the Little Colonel, only crosser. I have a friend named Alan Campbell who is also a Sara-and-Gerald-Murphy fan and we often exchange letters. I have two Bedlington terriers and a dachshund, none of which is housebroken, so you can see I am pretty busy — My hobby is the hives, which I have had ever since setting foot on California soil. I scratch a great deal, which has won me the title of Miss Glamour of 1935. It is very pretty here and I like it very much, all except my work at the studio, which stinks.

Well, I must close now, as Fraulein, the dachshund, has just done everything but have her puppies on the white carpet which her host and hostess went without eating for a month in order to acquire. She is a very cute little dog, if only she would stop going to the bathroom for five consecutive minutes, and sends love.

I wish I was this letter, so I could go in a plane and be with you *quick*.

Dorothy—

The back of the envelope bears a Paramount Picture insignia under the following inscription: "If it's a Paramount Picture it's the best show in town!" Underneath Parker wrote: "This is an outrageous lie."

"...naturally she can't
turn up back at work
plus a baby..."

𝓕RIENDSHIP IS DEFINED in many ways. Sometimes it is what we are willing to give a friend. At other times it is what we are willing to ask of a friend. For Dorothy Sayers it was both. Not only was Dorothy Sayers willing to give, but she was comfortable and confident enough to make the ultimate request of her best friend, her cousin Ivy Shrimpton.

Throughout Dorothy's life she wrote letters to her cousin. To Ivy she confessed her schoolgirl crushes and later her romances. The most significant of those romances was with an American writer who was opposed to bringing children into the world and who professed no interest in marriage. She, however, wanted marriage and children, and she would not agree to an affair.

Her would-be suitor then went to the United States and married a widowed mother of two. Stunned and hurt, Dorothy subsequently had a brief affair with an unemployed motor mechanic whom she scarcely knew. Her true revenge, however, came in a far better way. She created a character based on her American—and killed him.

Meanwhile Cousin Ivy and her widowed mother earned their living by caring for foster children.

Dorothy's fame came as a poet, a translator of Dante, a Christian writer, and creator of first-class detective stories whose protagonist was Lord Peter Wimsey. In addition to her considerable literary output, the one thing Dorothy Sayers never failed to write was letters—letters to her family, to her friends—and especially to her cousin and best friend Ivy, the one person of whom she could make any request.

24 Great James St.
W.C. 1

Dearest Ivy

Thank you very much indeed for your letter. . . . I have been wanting for some time to write to you on a matter of business. There's an infant I'm very anxious you should have the charge of, and I hope very much indeed you'll be able to take it. It isn't actually there yet, but will be before many days are over. It won't have any legal father, poor little soul, but I know you would be all the more willing to help give it the best possible start in life on that account. The parents want to do the very best for it, and will be ready and willing to pay whatever your usual terms are, and probably something over. They especially want it to have affection rather than pomp! I know that nobody could do better for it that way than you. I am very personally interested in the matter, and will tell you more about it later on, or when I see you as I hope to do before too long. The point is—what would be the earliest possible moment at which you could take it? At present everything depends on the girl's not losing her job. Everything has been most discreetly managed—her retirement from public life is accounted for by "illness"—but naturally she can't turn up back at work plus a baby—at least, not without letting stacks and stacks of people into the secret, which might then leak out. So you see, the sooner she could dump the infant on you and clear back to work, the more chance there [is] of there being money to support it, and both parents are working— one of them alone couldn't do much to support it. From the mother's history it should be an extremely healthy child, having given not the slightest trouble or bad time so far, and I understand the doctor thinks everything should go easily. It will be a little gent (or lady as the case may be) on both sides, and would probably be in your charge for some years—till circumstances enable the mother to take it herself. I think you would find it a paying proposition, and I do very much hope that you will be able to help in the matter, as I feel that nobody could do better for it than you. Indeed, I'd ask you to make a very special effort in the matter—it is so great a relief to feel that somebody really trustworthy will have the child,—its mother is counting much on my cousin!

Please let me know by return of post whether you can manage it by hook or by crook—and if so, the earliest moment at which you could take it, and what your terms would be. I can guarantee the payments—and you would be given an entirely free hand in such matters as doctors, clothing, and necessaries of every kind.

I am rather in a hurry as usual, so can only say how glad I am you like Lord Peter. There will be a new adventure of his very soon . . .

My very best love to Aunt Amy—and don't fail us over the baby!

Your loving
Dorothy

Tuckton Lodge
Southbourne
Hampshire
27 January 1924

Dearest Ivy —

I am bringing the boy to you myself on Wednesday. Owing to the strike, we shall probably have to come by road, so expect us at your door some time in the afternoon. As I shall try to get up to town by train the same night I may only be able to stay a minute or two so am enclosing confidential particulars which I had intended to give you by word of mouth. I know you are the most discreet woman in the world — will you read them first yourself, and only tell Aunt Amy about it if, on consideration, you think fit. I trust your discretion absolutely.

Yours
affectionately
Dorothy

[Letter enclosed. On envelope]: STRICTLY CONFIDENTIAL
Particulars about Baby
27 January 1924

My dear — Everything I told you about the boy is absolutely true — only I didn't tell you he was my own! — I won't go into the whole story — think the best you can of me — I know it won't make you love the boy any the less. He is really a fine little chap, — I can't feel too bad about it myself now, because

171

it will be so jolly to have him later on. I'm 30 now, and it didn't seem at all likely I should marry—and I shall have something for my latter age anyway. But never mind me—don't think about it, but just be fond of the little chap. I wouldn't like to send him to anybody but you, because I know I can trust you absolutely to give him everything which I can't give him these first years.

I didn't tell you straight away for two reasons: l. I thought you would be able to tell me more frankly about terms, and whether it would be convenient for you to have him, if you thought he was someone else's. 2. I have no idea what Aunt Amy will feel about it. If you think it would distress her very much there is no need to tell her—you have a quite plausible story to account for my interest in him. Please use your own judgement. Whatever you do will be right.

They know nothing about it at home, and they must know nothing. It would grieve them quite unnecessarily. You know, it's not the kind of ill-doing that Mother has any sympathy for,—she isn't a man-lover or a baby-worshipper,—so I see no reason whatever for distressing them. So please, not a word of any kind to Christchurch. By the time I want the boy, they will be too old, if they are still alive, to worry much about anything, and they must have these last years in peace. I know you can be as silent as the grave, and I trust you to be so in this case.

The boy will have to be registered in my name, of course, but I think he may as well be known by his father's, which is as noncommittal and common as blackberries—so to you and the world he'll be John Anthony White. For certain reasons, that isn't the name I'm using here [the maternity home], so I haven't been able to mark his things.

I'm afraid you'll have a job with him at first—food, etc.,— because he has been breast-fed. They said it would be better to give him a good start in the natural way and then let him struggle with the change of food than to bottle-feed him from the beginning. He is very greedy and seems to have a pretty sturdy little inside, so I hope you'll be able to get him started without too much trouble. You will know what to try. If you need anything more expensive, or doctors or advice, or anything in the world for him, let me know. I can manage it.—He is rather noisy and excitable—you'll find it doesn't do to nurse him or pet him too much, or he'll keep you at it all day and night. He's accustomed to be stuck down in bed when he yowls and taken no notice of—so be stern with him.

He has been circumcised, by the doctor's advice, and I think you will find his little insides in good working order.

I'll tell you anything else there's time for when I see you.

> Good-bye till
> then, my dear—
> and be good to
> my son!
> Dorothy

"... I ... long to lay my weary head somewhere and nestle my full soul close to that of another in full sympathy —"

$\mathcal{S}$USAN B. ANTHONY and Elizabeth Cady Stanton sustained a friendship that lasted for forty years, yet through the years and despite their closeness Susan Anthony always addressed her closest friend as "Mrs. Stanton." It was Susan B. Anthony who created the first women's movement in the United States as she crusaded tirelessly for a woman's right to vote and campaigned vigorously for equal rights. She befriended many on her tireless route to freedom for women; she was a faithful diarist, a passionate letter writer, and a caring friend.

Appropriately, Stanton and Anthony—who were both

committed to their common cause, suffrage for women—met in 1851 on a street corner in Seneca Falls, New York. Anthony was then thirty-one, a tall and serious spinster, and Stanton, thirty-five, a witty and warm mother of seven.

Although the two women did not always travel together, they kept one another informed about their activities. This letter, written in 1857, is typical of their mutual expressions of affection and dedication.

Dear Mrs. Stanton

How I do long to be with you this very minute—to have one look into your very soul & one sound of your soul stirring voice—

I did hope to call on you before embarking on this Western voyage—but . . . opportunity came not— . . . That Convention has been a heavy burden to me, the last two months—nothing looking promising—nobody seemed to feel any personal responsibility and, *alone,*—feeling utterly incompetent I go forward, unless sure of reliable and effective speakers to sustain the Con.; I could but grope in the dark—but I now hope Lucy [Stone] will say *amen* to my proposition—

. . . Mrs. Stanton, I have *very weak* moments—and long to lay my weary head somewhere and nestle my full soul close to that of another in full sympathy—I sometimes fear that I *too* shall faint by the wayside—and drop out of the ranks of the faithful few—

There is so much, amid all that is so hopeful, to discourage & dishearten—and I feel *alone*. Still to know I am *not alone*, but that all the true & the good souls, both in & out of the body, keep me company, and that the good Father more than all is ever a host to every good effort—

But you will see that this is one of my tired moments—so no more, but to the Cause thereof . . .

*"... I kept thinking of
Iowa—of the cornhusking,
the snow, the sleighrides, the
coasting, skating, the evenings
with stories and popcorn and
nuts and apples..."*

$\mathcal{N}$EXT TIME YOU hear someone wax nostalgic over "the good old days," here's a letter you might want to share. It was written by a young Iowa farm woman, Elizabeth (Bess) Corey. Born in 1887, she was the eldest in a family of seven children who lived with their parents in a four-room house. Small wonder that Bess, when a teenager, quit high school, went to Normal School for a summer session and, like the Brontës and Jane Austen, began a career as a teacher boarding with neighbor families in the towns near her home. The similarity to the English teacher/writers ends there, however.

Bess's life was a hard one. In 1909 she left her overcrowded family home and set out for South Dakota to stake a claim, homestead the land, and teach. Her single continuing tie to family and friends were her letters.

As was the custom, Bess wrote her letters to her mother, and her mother would gather the family around the dining table and read the latest news from her daughter.

Bess complained, complimented, and teased—and her letters are filled with friendship and love.

What made a young woman leave her friends and family and go forth into the wilderness? The same thing that lured the Gold Rush prospectors—the promise of untold riches. In Bess's case, the riches were promised by the railroads who were trying to promote an expanded system. And so seventeen-year-old Bess went to make her claim, build a shack, find friends, and seek a job as a teacher.

Bess was no little lady; she stood five feet seven inches tall and weighed 180 pounds. Described as a "people person," Bess was not bashful. Still, to her mother (who, as did most friends, both delighted and irritated her), she confessed her loneliness, her uncertainty over boyfriends and finally her resolution to stay single. That the family learned when she began signing her letters "Bachelor Bess," which she later shortened to B.B.

The following letter is a typical one, for although Bess was involved in her community, obviously her greatest pleasure was getting and receiving letters from home. And when she longed for home, there was just one person to tell—"Ma."

Nov. 19, 1911/Fort Pierre, So. Dak.

Dear Ma, — Your card of Nov 4th reached here shortly before your letter — some one got the mail and left it at Browns barn in Ft Pierre so its a wonder I got it at all.

. . . A week ago Friday I had an attack of something the like of which I never had before. I just couldn't keep my mind on my work for the life of me — I kept thinking of Iowa — of the cornhusking, the snow, the sleighrides, the coasting, skating, the evenings with stories and popcorn and nuts and apples, the Xmas time, the spring when it is breaking up and the creek is out and later when every thing is green and we are putting in garden, taking care of little chick[s] and pigs and things and summer when the boys play ball in the creek pasture and then when we are putting up fruit and stuff and getting things in the cellar and — oh everything and my throat ached and I could hardly hear the classes recite. I don't know what you call it but its a bad dose and lasted an hour or so. That night we were to attend the good bye party for Emmie Lou but the weather was so cold and threatening we didn't go and weren't we glad we hadn't gone when we awoke next morning with that old blizzard a howling! It began Friday night and lasted till Sunday morning. I didn't suffer much as I did nothing but hug the stove to keep warm. The folks moved their beds down into the sitting room so we just about all live in one room as there is but the curtain between. Gee but that was a storm! Some folks haven't found all their stock yet that was driven through the fences. They say there were

179

about five hundred head of cattle in the streets of Pierre Sunday morning . . . Poor dazed frightened creatures.

. . . I am helping prepair a program for December 5th. We have a week off next week—am to attend the State Teachers Association meeting in Pierre. I'm trying to do some sewing and mending—also have another pair of . . . socks to knot.

I take three current events papers, three educational papers beside the *McCall* Magazine.

We attended the Farmers Protective Association meeting last Friday. They want me to join that but oh gee! I've got enough on deck now.

The Literary Society is to prepair a program for Xmas. That means more work for me too.

. . . You must take care of your self what ever happens.

. . . Had a good letter from Mary [an Iowa friend] the other day. Must close.

Lovingly yours
Bachelor Bess

"... it would be impossible for me not to want you as a friend."

$\mathcal{M}$ARYAT LEE, a playwright living in New York, really didn't want to meet Flannery O'Connor, "that lady writer," when she went home to visit in Midgeville, Georgia. But a friend intervened, and late in her visit of December 1956, Flannery telephoned and invited Maryat for an afternoon visit.

So began the funny, tender friendship between "the lady playwright" and "the lady writer."

When, the following year, Maryat wrote that she was going to Japan, Flannery asked playfully for "one saber-toothed tiger (with cub) and a button off Mao's jacket and any chickens that you see that I don't have already." And when Maryat described early details of her trip, Flannery responded with, "I daresay that being alone in Yokohama for you is equivalent to negotiating passage through the Chicago airport for me. There they also speak a foreign tongue."

But Flannery's own high spirits evidently backfired because in October, sounding suddenly conciliatory, Flannery O'Connor wrote this letter to Maryat Lee, a woman who was destined to remain her friend for the rest of Flannery's short life.

Flannery O'Connor, born in 1925, died in 1964. She battled lupus for years, but despite her physical ups and downs, she managed to write many letters every day.

8 October 57

I was much cheered and relieved to hear from you though the vein was mysterious. I haven't received any crusty note. Maybe you didn't put enough postage on it and it's simmering on the high seas; anyway, if you sent it, I reckon I provoked it. I scrounged around in my trash system trying to find if I had a carbon of my last to you. I had, and reading it over, found it in part disagreeable, vain, and unclear. I take it at this point to have been one of my attempts to be funny. It was not, but was as I saw with horror open to many possible interpretations of a vulgar nature. None of these was intended so put it down to my native idiocy. I just don't have a highly developed sensibility and I don't know when I've hurt people until they tell me. To have caused you any pain is very painful to me and is the last thing I would have wanted to do, or to have seemed to doubt for an instant that you ever act in any way not according to your conscience.

The only thing that irked me about the last letter I did get from you was your use of the word eternity in the plural, with airless in front of it. I don't mind being a pathetic quaver but eternity means the beatific vision to me and my quaver, or anybody else's, has nothing to do with it. Anyway, it would be impossible for me not to want you as a friend. A ridiculous notion. I am not to be got rid of by crusty letters. I'm as insult-proof as my buff orpington hen and if the letter ever does show up, I doubtless won't know the difference. . . .

"... never, never did I love you better,
all my beloved ones, than when
I left you —"

No ONE NEEDED supportive sisters more than Elizabeth Barrett. When Robert Browning fell in love with her and first came calling, he met a formidable enemy in Edward Moulton-Barrett, the father of the family, who had inherited great wealth and opposed marriage for all his children.

Despite her father's distinct displeasure over Mr. Browning, Elizabeth Barrett, although thirty and practically an invalid, managed to conduct a romance with the young poet (he was six years her junior) for a year and a half. Her sisters were always aware of the love of the two poets, and in this letter—her first to her sisters Henrietta and Arabel following the couple's secret wedding and departure for Florence—Elizabeth reaffirms their sisterly love and friendship.

Her father never forgave her for marrying and never spoke to her again.

Roanne
October 2, 1846

I thank and bless you my dearest Henrietta and Arabel . . . my own dearest kindest sisters!—what I suffered in reaching Orleans,—at last holding all these letters in my hands, can only be measured by my deep gratitude to you, and by the tears and kisses I spent upon every line of what you wrote to me . . . dearest kindest that you are . . . Robert brought in a great packet of letters. . . . and I held them in my hands, not able to open one, and growing paler and colder every moment . . .

They were very hard letters, those from dearest Papa and dearest George [her brother]—To the first I had to bow my head—I do not seem to myself to have deserved that full cup, in the intentions of this act—but he is my father and he takes his own view, of course, of what is before him to judge of. But for George, I thought it hard, I confess, that he should have written to me so with a sword. To write to me as if I did not love you all, — I who would have laid down my life at a sign, if it could have benefitted one of you really and essentially: — with the proof, you should have had life and happiness at a sign.

It was hard that he should use his love for me to half break my heart with such a letter — Only he wrote in excitement and ignorance. I ask of God to show to him and the most unbelieving of you, that never, never did I love you better, all my beloved ones, than when I left you — than in that day, and that moment . . .

Now I will tell you — Robert who had been waiting at the door, I believe, in great anxiety about me, came in and found me just able to cry from the balm of your tender words — I put your two letters into his hands, and he, when he had read them, said with tears in his eyes, and kissing them between the words — "I love your sisters with a deep affection — I am inexpressibly grateful to them, — It shall be the object of my life to justify this trust, as they express it here". . .

Dearest Henrietta and Arabel, — how I suffered that day — that miserable Saturday [September 12, 1846, the day of the wedding] . . . when I had to act a part to you — how I suffered! and how I had to think to myself that if I betrayed one pang of all, I should involve you deeply in the grief which otherwise remained my own. And Arabel to see through it, notwithstanding! I was afraid of her — she looked at me so intently, and was so grave . . . my dearest, dearest Arabel! Understand both of you, that if, from the apparent necessities of the instant, I consented to let the ceremony precede the departure by some few days, it was upon the condition of not seeing him again [in] that house and till we went away.

We parted, as we met, at the door of Marlyebone Church — he helped me at the communion table, and not a word passed after. I looked like death, he has said since. You see we were afraid of a sudden removal preventing everything . . . or at least, laying the unpleasantness on me of a journey to London previous to the ceremony, which particularly I should have hated, for very obvious reasons. There was no elopement in the case, but simply a private marriage . . . What I suffered under your eyes, you may guess — it was in proportion to every effort successfully made to disguise the suffering. Painful it is to look back upon now — Forgive me whatever was expiated in the deepest of my heart.

. . . No one can judge of this act, except some one who knows thoroughly the man I have married. He rises on me hour by hour. If ever a being of a higher order lived among us with a glory round his head, in these latter days, he is such a being.

Papa thinks that I have sold my soul — for genius . . . mere genius. Which I might have done when I was younger, if I had had the opportunity . . . but am in no danger of doing now. For my sake, for the love of me, from an infatuation which from first to last has astonished me, he has consented to occupy for a moment a questionable position.

But those who question most, will do him justice fullest — and we must wait a little with resignation. In the meanwhile, what he is, and what he is to me, I would fain teach you. — Have faith in me to believe it. He puts out all his great faculties to give me pleasure and comfort . . . charms me into thinking of him when he sees my thoughts wandering . . . forces me to smile in spite of all of them . . .

. . . And he loves me more and more. Today we have been together a fortnight, and he said to me with a deep, serious tenderness . . . "I kissed your feet, my Ba, before I married you — but now I would kiss the ground under your feet, I love you with so much greater love." And this is true. I see and feel. I feel to have the power to make him happy . . . I feel to have it in my hands. It is strange that anyone so brilliant should love me, — but true and strange it is . . . and it is impossible for me to doubt it any more. Perfectly happy therefore we should be, if I could look back on you all without this pang.

. . . But I think . . . think . . . of the suffering I caused you, my own, own Arabel, that evening! I tremble thinking of you that evening — my own dearest dearest Arabel! Oh, do not fancy that new affections can undo the old. I love you now even more, I think. Robert is going to write to you from Pisa, and to Henrietta also. He loves you as his sisters . . .

. . . I am going to write to Papa — and to George — very soon, I shall. Ah — dear George would not have written so, if he had known my whole heart, yet he loved me while he wrote, as I felt with very pain the writing caused me. Dear George, — I love him to his worth. And my poor Papa! My thoughts cling to you all, and will not leave their hold. Dearest Henrietta and Arabel let me be as ever and for ever

Your fondly
attached
Ba

"When [women] fail,
then failure must be but a
challenge to others."

$\mathscr{A}$MELIA EARHART WAS born long before women spoke in their own true voices, and during her life she managed not only to flaunt the times but to challenge forever our automatic assumptions about what women can or cannot do. A midwesterner born in Kansas, she was educated at Columbia and Harvard; in 1928 she joined two American pilots, Wilmer Stultz and Louis Gordon, on a transatlantic flight and became the first woman to make the crossing by air. Having reached that goal, Amelia Earhart decided that her next would be a formidable one; she would be the first woman to fly the Atlantic alone. She not only succeeded, but established a new record: 13 hours and 30 minutes.

She was married to the publisher George Palmer Putnam, and some suspect that it was at his prodding that she made her last flight with less than adequate equipment.

What we do know for certain is that she wrote letters and kept diaries and journals.

Her disappearance on that Pacific flight in 1937 has been the basis for much political and romantic speculation, but the lines that follow here are not supposition. They are words she wrote just before that fatal flight—and they were addressed to her husband—just in case.

. . . Please know I am quite aware of the hazards.

I want to do it because I want to do it. Women must try to do things as men have tried. When they fail, then failure must be but a challenge to others.

courage

Courage is the price that life exacts for granting
   peace.
The soul that knows it not, knows no release
From little things;

Knows not the livid loneliness of fear
Nor mountain heights, where bitter joy can hear
The sound of wings.

How can life grant us boon of living, compensate
For dull gray ugliness and pregnant hate
Unless we dare

The soul's dominion? each time we make a
   choice, we pay
With courage to behold resistless day
And count it fair.

*"How you men wriggle
and twist, and turn your
backs on all logic, before
you will recognise the truth."*

ON SOME WAYS their story paralleled that of Robert
Browning and Elizabeth Barrett, whose father disapproved
of her marrying, but Robert Schumann and Clara Wieck had
a happier ending. Clara's father, who taught music to both his
daughter and the man who later became her husband, opposed their marriage on the grounds that Schumann was not
sufficiently gifted. When he was later proved wrong, he
wrote a letter to his daughter (by then not only married but
also a mother) asking to come to hear the next concert at
which Schumann's work would be played. And from that
time on, he was a part of their lives.

Like so many women of her time, however, Clara Schumann subordinated her own considerable talent as a concert pianist to that of her composer husband. His intimate friends, and the ones who peopled her life, were Mendelssohn, Joachim, Liszt, Chopin, and Brahms. She was the first to play Beethoven's *Appassionata* in a concert hall and studied Bach when he was an unknown.

Brahms sent his "things" to her after they were written, and she commented on them. The *Ave Maria*, she wrote in November 1859, "with its wonderfully touching simplicity must sound exquisite." But Clara was no simple sycophant as this letter proves. She was forthright in her roles as daughter, wife, mother, and artist. After the death of her husband, she was left with seven children under the age of fifteen and, as a result, concertized with more frequency in order to earn a living.

Kreuznach, Sept. 16th 1860

Dearest Johannes

What a magnificent surprise you have given me! What beautiful compositions! How glad I am at last to be able to play the D minor variations [printed later as the second movement of the first sextet] for myself. . . .

But where shall I begin? How difficult it is to set down everything shortly and clearly in black and white, when one has as little power of expression as I have, words always seem so feeble compared with what I feel. Feeling is so many-sided, and words have but one side. If one is sitting beside anyone, one can point out each note that one likes or dislikes, and how much pleasanter that is.

Once more you have found your way into the depths of art, e.g., in the double canon, which I contemplate with more amazement than comfort, for here and there it sounds to me stiff, as indeed it can hardly help being, in such a form. The prelude must sound well, but it worries me that the crotchet figure ceases so abruptly. . . . the entrance of the chorus is extremely beautiful, but the harmony becomes stiff. . . . later it becomes beautiful again. Also in the transition to the first prelude; c,b,c, in the bass hurts me however much I try to make it sound by using the pedal. The *Amen* sounds well, but is it not rather long in relation to the whole? No doubt the organ brings out much that sounds dry on the piano. . . . the E in the tenor at the end disturbs me, it sounds so thick; why do you not substitute F sharp? I could very well spare the sev-

enth, it sounds rather modern in this place. The fugue is beautiful, so skillful and at the same time so melodious (except in a few places).

. . . I cannot help laughing at what you say about the "illogical" and "unnecessary" things that I write sometimes. How you men wriggle and twist, and turn your backs on all logic, before you will recognise the truth. What I wrote to you referred only to myself. You had been living for two months with Joachim in beautiful surroundings; had I not a right to wish for, and claim one of them at least? That I saw you for only a few days is a fact which cannot be explained away, but it seemed to me quite right that you should go to Hamburg after knocking about for so long, even if there was no denying that if you had wished to see me again you could easily have come over here, and by so doing you would have given me a pleasure. But I mention this only with reference to the logic. . . .

Postscript

One thing I have learned through researching and writing this book is that while some memories may prove painful, the absence of memories is more painful still. As is the way of many writers, I talked with friends and associates during the time I worked on the book (who knew where a good letter was hiding?). Most people bemoaned the lack of letters in today's world. But their eyes also lit up as the word "letters" revived poignant moments of life.

To find the letters for this book I made use of libraries and bookshops, and I want to offer my special thanks and appreciation to the New York Society Library, which turned out to be a treasure trove for much of what I needed. I also combed the stacks of the East Hampton Library and was helped by the diligent staff there. My bookshop friends came to my aid, too, especially the wonderful staff at Bookhampton in East Hampton, and the people at the Doubleday store at Fifty-seventh Street and Fifth Avenue in New York. Thanks to my loving friends Annelle Warwick Savitt, Phyllis Cerf Wagner, Faith Brunson, Marciarose Shestack, Patricia Rosenwald, Eva Pusta, Marianne Gogolick, Kasper and Sandra Kasper, Eunice Podis Weiskopf, Helene Silver, Peter Rogers, Corky Ribakoff, Betty Rollin, John Mack Carter, Phyllis Levy, Jeffrey Butler, and Hope Gropper. Thanks also to Cindy Greenfield, my efficient and caring assistant, Margot Adams, and Owen Laster, my helpful friend and agent. As always, thanks to my family: Heidi and Zev Guber; Denise and Robert Wyse; Katherine Wyse Goldman, my literary friend and counselor and my darling daughter; her husband Henry Goldman; and Kenneth Wyse. Once again I had the special joy of working with Laurie Bernstein, an editor whose heart is *sympatico* and whose advice is direct and expert. Her professional and personal insights have strengthened our friendship and helped immeasurably in shaping this book. I am grateful also to many of her associates at Simon & Schuster, particularly Carolyn Reidy, Michele Martin, Bonni Leon-Berman, Amy Hill, Larry Norton, Anne Hughes, and Paula Munck, whose beautiful art has enhanced the book.

In the midst of working on this book, I didn't really think I would have to cope with moving my home. But I did. And then a couple of weeks after the routing and rerouting of my past, the real estate agent called. "We've found a couple of metal file cabinets in the basement of the old house. What do you want us to do with them?"

My first reaction was to throw them away. God, after moving a house and barn, who needs to find more stuff to sift and sort? But then I remembered. Those must have been my husband's files, the files sent from Lee's office after he died — the files I'd so easily ordered to the basement. Now they were about to be exhumed.

I guess exhumed is the right word when long-dead papers turn up to tease the living. And, in a way, exhuming is what I've been doing with this book. I've been digging into the pasts of many people who have been dead so long that no one still remembers them as live characters on life's stage.

Reluctantly I went into the files of my late husband.

Much of what I found was as boring as I expected: old insurance forms, receipts, tax returns. Some of it was painful: the medical reports on what turned out to be Lee's last illness, notes about the deaths of his parents. And some is to be treasured forever: his college diploma, army commission, our wedding license, even the menu from our wedding dinner.

Like the letters in this book, these mementos validated experience and life because someone cared enough to write about them and, more importantly, to save them and to treasure them. It seemed almost providential that in the midst of this book these reminders of him and of our life together came to me.

In the file in Lee's cabinet marked "Lois" was a typewritten note on my office stationery with some lines my friend Bill Bernbach once quoted, lines Lee had asked me to send.

I am including the little quatrain here, for even though this is a collection of letters written by women, the words of men also humor us and touch our hearts:

> while you and i have eyes and lips
> which are for seeing and to kiss with
> who cares if some one-eyed sonofabitch
> invents an instrument to measure spring with

Lee had also saved every note with every gift I ever gave him. I reread them and relived the moments we had celebrated. And I thought of how much I missed him.

But it wasn't until I came across an undated note I'd sent that I realized in my own heart that what makes a woman's letters truly special is timelessness.

And so I read these words only a woman would write, a letter sent before we had decided to marry, a time when we'd had a separation of some kind (his idea or mine? who can remember? my guess is that it was at his instigation).

It was written on my stationery in my hand and read:

There's a very big hole in my life where once you were—and no matter where I turn nothing fills the space the way you do.

I do not know why some things work and some do not. I know only that with you everything in my life seems to work better.

For the first time in years I'm aware of being left-handed in a right-handed world. I miss you.

Lois

I read the words again and again.

Because through my tears I had found the old, remembered truth of our relationship.

Only a saved letter could have told me.

Thank you, Lee. Once again, thank you.

Bibliography

Berliner, Michael S., ed. *Letters of Ayn Rand*. New York: Penguin Books USA, Dutton, 1995.

Bertholf, Robert J., ed. *A Great Admiration: H.D. and Robert Duncan Correspondence, 1950–1961*. Venice, Cal.: The Lapis Press, 1992.

Brightman, Carol, ed. *Between Friends: The Correspondence of Hannah Arendt and Mary McCarthy, 1949–1975*. San Diego, Cal.: Harcourt Brace & Company, Harvest Book, 1996.

Butterfield, L. H., Marc Friedlander, and Mary-Jo Kline, eds. *The Book of Abigail and John: Selected Letters of the Adams Family, 1762–1784*. Cambridge, Mass.: Harvard University Press, 1975.

Cott, Nancy F., ed. *A Woman Making History: Mary Ritter Beard Through Her Letters*. New Haven, Conn.: Yale University Press, 1991.

Dillon, Millicent, ed. *Out In the World: Selected Letters of Jane Bowles, 1935–1970*. Santa Rosa, Calif.: Black Sparrow Press, 1985.

Everett, Patricia R., ed. *A History of Having a Great Many Times Not Continued to Be Friends: The Correspondence Between Mabel Dodge and Gertrude Stein, 1911–1934*. Albuquerque, N.M.: University of New Mexico Press, 1996.

Fisher, M.F.K. *Stay Me, Oh Comfort Me: Journals and Stories, 1933–1941.* New York: Pantheon Books, 1993.

Fitzgerald, Sally, ed., *Flannery O'Connor: The Habit of Being.* New York: Farrar, Straus and Giroux, 1979.

Freeman, Martha, ed. *Always Rachel: The Letters of Rachel Carson and Dorothy Freeman, 1952–1964.* Boston: Beacon Press, 1995.

Gerber, Philip L., ed. *Bachelor Bess: The Homesteading Letters of Elizabeth Corey, 1909–1919.* Iowa City, Iowa: University of Iowa Press, 1990.

Giroux, Robert, ed. *One Art: Elizabeth Bishop Letters.* New York: Farrar, Straus and Giroux, 1994.

Haight, Gordon S., ed., *The George Eliot Letters,* 6 vols. London: Oxford University Press, 1954.

Hanff, Helene. *84, Charing Cross Road.* New York: Grossman Publishers, 1970; New York: Penguin Books, 1990.

Hedrick, Joan D., ed. *Harriet Beecher Stowe: A Life.* New York: Oxford University Press, 1994.

Hour of Gold, Hour of Lead: Diaries and Letters of Anne Morrow Lindbergh, 1929–1932. New York: Harcourt Brace Jovanovich, 1973.

Lash, Joseph P., ed. *Love, Eleanor: Eleanor Roosevelt and Her Friends.* New York: Doubleday, 1982.

Lehmann, John and Derek Parker, eds. *Edith Sitwell: Selected Letters,* London: Macmillan, 1970.

Lewis, R.W.B., and Nancy Lewis, eds. *Letters of Edith Wharton.* New York: Scribner's, 1988.

Litoff, Judy Barrett, and David K. Smith, eds. *Since You Went Away: World War II Letters from American Women on the Home Front.* New York: Oxford University Press, 1991.

Litzmann, Berthold, ed. *Clara Schumann: An Artist's Life.* Vol. 2. Translated and abridged from the 4th ed. by Grace E. Hadow. London: Macmillan, 1913.

Macdougall, Allan Ross, ed. *Letters of Edna St. Vincent Millay*. New York: Harper & Brothers, 1952.

Miller, Linda Patterson, ed. *Letters from the Lost Generation: Gerald and Sara Murphy and Friends*. New Brunswick, N.J.: Rutgers University Press, 1991.

Mosley, Charlotte, ed. *Love from Nancy: The Letters of Nancy Mitford*. Boston: Houghton Mifflin Co., 1993.

Nicolson, Nigel, ed. *The Letters of Virginia Woolf*, Vol. 4, *1929–1931*. San Diego, Cal.: Harcourt Brace & Company, 1978. Originally published in England as *A Reflection of the Other Person*, Hogarth Press.

Phelps, Robert, ed. *Letters from Colette*. New York: Farrar, Straus and Giroux, 1980.

Reynolds, Barbara, ed. *The Letters of Dorothy Sayers*. New York: St. Martin's Press, 1996.

Schuster, Lincoln M., ed. *A Treasury of the World's Greatest Letters*. New York: Simon & Schuster, 1940.

Sher, Lynn, ed. *Failure Is Impossible: Susan B. Anthony in Her Own Words*. New York: Random House, Times Books, 1995.

Sherline, Reid, ed. *Letters Home*. New York: Timken Publishers, 1993.

Taylor, Judy, and Frederick Warne, eds. *Beatrix Potter's Letters*. London: The Penguin Group, 1989.

Vicinus, Martha, and Bea Nergaard, eds. *Ever Yours: Florence Nightingale, Selected Letters*. Cambridge, Mass.: Harvard University Press, 1990.

War Within and Without: Diaries and Letters of Anne Morrow Lindbergh, 1939–1944. Orlando, Fla.: Harcourt Brace and Co., 1980.

(continued from copyright, page 4)

Beacon Press for excerpts from *Always Rachel* edited by Martha Freeman. Copyright © 1995 by Martha Freeman. Black Sparrow Press for a letter dated May 10, 1966 by Jane Bowles. Copyright © 1985 by Paul Frederic Bowles. Reprinted from *Out in the World: Selected Letters of Jane Bowles*. Blackwell Publishers for excerpts from *The Brontes; Their Lives, Friendships, and Correspondences*, Vols i-iii, eds. T. J. Wise and J. A. Symington (pub The Shakespeare Head Press). Nancy F. Cott and the Schlessinger Library, Radcliffe College for a letter from Mary Ritter Beard to Luella Gettys from *A Woman Making History* edited by Nancy F. Cott (Yale University Press, 1991.) David Highman Associates for an excerpt from *Edith Sitwell: Selected Letters*, ed. John Lehmann and Derek Parker (London: MacMillian 1970). Doubleday, a division of Bantam Doubleday Dell Publishing Group, Inc. for excerpts from *Love Eleanor, Eleanor Roosevelt and Her Friends*: by Joseph P. Lash, Doubleday, 1982 . Dutton Signet, a division of Penguin Books, USA, and Michael Berlinger for "July 26, 1945 Letters to Isabel Paterson", from *Letters of Ayn Rand*, Michael Berlinger, editor. Copyright © 1995 by The Estate of Ayn Rand. Introduction copyright © 1995 by Leonard Peikoff. The Estate of Gertrude Stein for excerpts from the correspondence between Mabel Dodge and Gertrude Stein, previously included in *A History of Having a Great Time Not Continue To Be Friends* by Patricia R. Everett (University of New Mexico Press, 1996). Farrar, Straus, & Giroux: Letter to Marianne Moore from *One Art* by Elizabeth Bishop. Copyright © 1994 by Alice Helen Methfessel. Letters to Marguerite Moreno from *Letters of Colette* by Colette. Translation copyright © 1980 by Robert Phelps. Excerpt from letter to Maryat Lee from *The Habit of Being* by Flannery O'Connor. Copyright © 1979 by Regina O'Connor. Harcourt Brace & Company for use of excerpts from *Hour of Gold, Hour of Lead: Diaries and Letters of Anne Morrow Lindbergh* 1929-1932, copyright © 1973 by Anne Morrow Lindbergh. Excerpt from the *Letters of Virginia Woolf*, Volume IV: 1929-1931 edited by Nigel Nicolson and Joanne Trautmann, copyright © 1978 by Quentin Bell and Angelica Garnett. Excerpts from *Between Friends: The Correspondence of Hannah Arendt and Mary McCarthy* 1949-1975, edited by Carol Brightman, copyright © 1995 by the Literary Trust of Hannah Arendt Blucher, Lotte Kohler, Trustee, copyright © 1995 by the Literary Trust of Mary McCarthy West, Margo Viscusi and Eve Stwertka, Trustees. Harvard University Press for an early 1878 letter from *The Letters of Emily Dickinson*, edited by Thomas H. Johnson, Cambridge, Mass.: The Belknap Press of Harvard University Press, copyright © 1958, 1986 by the President and Fellows of Harvard College and for a July 10, 1777 letter from *The Book of Abigail and John: Selected Letters of the Adams*, 1772-1784 edited and with an introduction by L. H. Butterfield, Marc Friedlander and Mary-Jo Kline, Cambridge, Mass.: Harvard University Press, copy-